THE TAFSĪR OF
SŪRAH NŪH

A COMMENTARY OF SŪRAH NŪH
[The 71ˢᵗ Chapter of the Glorious Qur'ān]

SHAYKH ABDUL RAHEEM LIMBĀDĀ

ḤAFIẒAHULLĀH

Tafseer-Raheemi Publications 2022
Info@tafseer-raheemi.com

First Edition: March 2007
Second Revised Edition: Dhul Qaa'dā 1438/August 2017
Third Edition: Sha'ban 1443 / March 2022
ISBN: 978-1-912301-02-7

Author	Shaykh Abdul Raheem Limbādā
	(www.tafseer-raheemi.com)
Cover Design	Mufti Abdul-Rahmān Mangera
	(www.zamzamacademy.com)
Typesetting	Belal Isakjee
Printed by	Elma Basim, Istanbul, Turkey

Other available titles in this series:

Available to purchase from www.tafseer-raheemi.com/shop

CONTENTS

PREFACE

In the name of Allāh ☫, the Most Compassionate, the Most Merciful. All praises belong to Allāh ☫, and benediction and salutation be upon the Imām of the Prophets and Messengers, and upon his entire household and all his companions.

The honourable and respectful Shaykh Abdul Raheem [Hāfizahullāh], prior to the present work, wrote a work of Qur'ānic exegesis on Sūrah Yūsuf, in English, which was exceedingly well received. Consequently, this raised his self-confidence and a further work of Qur'ānic exegesis on Sūrah Nūh has materialised.

The recitation of the Qur'ān and contemplation and reflection upon its verses is the loftiest form of servitude to Allāh ☫ [*Ibādah*], in particular as He, may His majesty be exalted, has recorded within the Qur'ān the episodes of past Messengers and civilisations, in order for the creation of Allāh ☫ to receive admonition. The success in both worlds for those who follow the noble Prophets and the severity and calamity upon those who reject them is repeatedly heralded within the Qur'ān. The most significant episode of these is the one of the Prophet Nūh ☫ and his community. The floods that came in the form of retribution, according to scholarly opinion, did not come upon merely one area, one country, or one particular region, but rather engulfed the whole of the earth.

May Allāh ☫ bestow this work with the honour of Divine endorsement and protect the human race from the heedlessness that prevails with regards to the punishment of Allāh ☫. We see that because of this sedated state, people are engrossed in rebellion against the injunctions of Allāh ☫. May Allāh ☫ guide us and protect us. Āmīn!

[Hadhrat Shaykh] Yūsuf Motālā ☫
Translated by Shaykh Mahmood Chāndia [Hāfizahullāh]

FOREWORD

Alhamdulillāh, I have known Shaykh Abdul Raheem [Hāfizahullāh] since childhood in both a personal and professional capacity. I am honoured to compliment a very comprehensive *tafsīr* of Sūrah Nūh from a very well respected and very hard-working scholar.

Shaykh Abdul Raheem has been teaching the sciences of *Hadīth* and *Qur'ān* at Darul Uloom Bury for many years under the guidance of Shaykh Hadhrat Maulānā Yūsuf Motālā [﷼], who instructed him to begin this project following his previous work on Sūrah Yūsuf.

Shaykh Abdul Raheem has produced a very well researched *tafsīr* of Sūrah Nūh and most importantly something that is understandable by all.

May Allāh ﷻ accept this work and reward Shaykh Abdul Raheem for his effort. May this be just the beginning of a whole chain of works from this respected scholar.

Inshā-Allāh, this work will bring further understanding of this popular sūrah, which in turn will increase the concentration and devotion when recited and heard in *salāh*, which is one of the aims of this project.

Wasalām

[Shaykh] Yūsuf Abdullāh Darwān [Hāfizahullāh]

AUTHOR'S FOREWORD

In the name of Allāh, the Most Compassionate the Most Merciful

A lhamdulillāh, by the grace of Allāh 🕌, the *tafsīr* of Sūrah Nūh was completed a long time ago. But it has taken some time for it to be published.

First, I would like to thank all my friends who helped me with checking and editing. Especially [Maulānā] Belal Isakjee, without whose help this would not have been possible.

Also I would like to thank my dearest friend and companion Shaykh Yūsuf Darwān for taking the time out for proofreading. We had some heart-warming discussions and he gave me some valuable suggestions for which I am very grateful.

Sister Āatika Bora also deserves special thanks, because in this day and age nobody wants to do anything for free, whereas she very wholeheartedly did proofreading and also gave valuable suggestions.

May Allāh 🕌 reward them all in this world as well as in the hereafter. Āmīn!

[Shaykh] Abdul Raheem Limbādā [Hāfizahullāh]

THE TAFSĪR OF SŪRAH NŪH

I was previously instructed by my Shaykh, Hadhrat Yūsuf Motālā [☙], to write the *tafsīr* of Sūrah Yūsuf. *Alhamdulillāh*, that was completed and is now available in the form of a book.

He has now instructed me to write the *tafsīr* of Sūrah Nūh. Many Imāms often recite this sūrah in Fajr salāh. If we listen to it while understanding the meaning, it might help us in concentrating and focusing on our *salāh*.

This sūrah was revealed in Makkāh Mukarramah. It consists of twenty-eight [28] verses, two-hundred and twenty-four [224] words, and nine-hundred and ninety-nine [999] letters. [1]

The contents of this sūrah are very similar to those of other Makkī sūrahs. *Tawhīd* has been explained and proven; *shirk*, polytheism and idol worship have been refuted.

The endeavours of Sayyidunā Nūh ☙ in calling his people towards Allāh ☙, his zeal for them to be guided, and his efforts to converse with them day and night, have been narrated to us. In spite of all this, they rejected Nūh ☙, showed their anger towards him, refused to look at his face and blocked their ears when he tried to say something. These incidents are related to us so that if we come across similar situations, we too can take solace from the Prophet's encounters. Another point to keep in mind is that the condition of our Prophet ☙ was very similar. So he would have found some comfort in reciting this sūrah too.

Prophets are human beings. It was natural for them to feel aggrieved by the hostility they were shown. When Nūh ☙ grew frustrated with his people after calling them for a period of nine hundred and fifty years [950], he could no longer tolerate their

---

[1] Khāzin.

obstinacy and he cursed them. Allāh's ﷻ wrath fell upon those people, the flood that wiped out that nation from the face of the Earth.

The only survivors were those who accepted the truth and followed Nūh ﷺ. He prayed for forgiveness for himself, his parents and his followers. [2]

---

[2] Mā'riful Qur'ān.

VERSE 1

اِنَّآ اَرْسَلْنَا نُوْحًا اِلٰى قَوْمِهٖٓ اَنْ اَنْذِرْ

قَوْمَكَ مِنْ قَبْلِ اَنْ يَّأْتِيَهُمْ عَذَابٌ اَلِيْمٌ ﴿١﴾

Indeed we sent Nūh to his people that 'Warn thy people
before there comes upon them a painful chastisement.'

"Indeed we sent Nūh..." Allāh ﷻ confirms that Nūh ﷺ was sent by Him
as a messenger. Nūh ﷺ was no ordinary person. He was a Rasūl of
Allāh ﷻ. A Rasūl is someone whom Allāh ﷻ sends to the creation in
order to convey the message of Allāh ﷻ. Allāh's ﷻ majesty, dignity,
and honour are such that it would not be appropriate for Him to
converse directly with every individual. However, He would not leave
the people without any form of guidance; therefore, He chose some
messengers from among the creation who would convey His message.
Each of Allāh's ﷻ messengers was rewarded for fulfilling their duty.

Being a messenger is not a quality that can be gained through
excessive worship. It is the prerogative of Allāh ﷻ to choose whom He
wills. Allāh ﷻ declares in the Qur'ān:

اَللّٰهُ يَجْتَبِىٓ اِلَيْهِ مَنْ يَّشَاءُ وَيَهْدِىٓ اِلَيْهِ مَنْ يُّنِيْبُ ۝

"Allāh chooses for Himself whomsoever He wills
and guides to Himself whoever turns [to Him]." [3]

Allāh ﷻ says:

اَللّٰهُ يَصْطَفِىْ مِنَ الْمَلٰٓئِكَةِ رُسُلًا وَّمِنَ النَّاسِ ۝

"Allāh chooses message deliverers, from the angels,

---

[3] Qur'ān 42:13.

and from the people." [4]

He ﷺ also says:

اَللّٰهُ اَعْلَمُ حَيْثُ يَجْعَلُ رِسَالَتَهٗ ۞

"Allāh knows very well where to place his message." [5]

In one Hadīth, Nūh ؑ is regarded among the prophets of great courage [Ulul-azm]. Nasafī says: 'Nūh in the Suryani [Syrriac] language means Al Sakin, the cool one.'

Ibn Kathīr narrates from Yazīd al Riqashī who says, 'He was named Nūh because he used to cry a lot over his condition.' [The word 'nawhah' means to cry upon the death of someone].

"To his nation..." Like all others Prophets [from the 124,000 Prophets sent by Allāh], Prophet Nūh ؑ was sent with a message for his nation only. All Prophets were regional, tribal, national. Only one Prophet was international, universal; that is Muhammad ﷺ.

One Hadīth in *Sahīh al-Bukhārī* states that our Prophet Muhammad ﷺ said:

فضلت على الانبياء بست : اوتيت بجوامع الكلم وجعلت لى الارض مسجدا وطهورا ونصرت بالرعب مسيرة شهر وكان النبي يبعث الى قومه خاصة وارسلت الى الخلق كافة وختم بى النبيون ـ

"I have been given preference over other Prophets in six ways: (i) I was given *Jawaami'ul Kalim* [complete and short words, suffused with meaning]. (ii) For me the whole earth was made a masjid [place of worship]. (iii) And made *tahoor* [For the purification, i.e. *Tayammum*]. (iv)

---

[4] Qur'ān 22:75.
[5] Qur'ān 6:124.

I was aided by the inspirational awe which permeates the distance of one month. (v) I was sent to the whole of creation, whereas other prophets were sent to their nations only. (vi) I was made the final Prophet [no prophet will be born after me]." [6]

Our Prophet Muhammad ﷺ was sent to the whole of mankind. The Qur'ān says:

$$\text{وَمَآ اَرْسَلْنٰكَ اِلَّا كَآفَّةً لِّلنَّاسِ بَشِيْرًا وَنَذِيْرًا}$$

$$\text{وَّلٰكِنَّ اَكْثَرَ النَّاسِ لَا يَعْلَمُوْنَ ۞}$$

"And We have not sent thee [O Muhammad], but as a bringer of good news and as a warner unto all mankind but most of mankind know not." [7]

The Qur'ān also says:

$$\text{وَمَآ اَرْسَلْنٰكَ اِلَّا رَحْمَةً لِّلْعٰلَمِيْنَ ۞}$$

"We did not send thee except as a mercy for all the worlds." [8]

One Hadīth says:

$$\text{وَكَانَ النَّبِيُّ يُبْعَثُ إِلَى قَوْمِهِ خَاصَّةً وَبُعِثْتُ إِلَى كُلِّ أَحْمَرَ وَأَسْوَدَ ۔}$$

"Every apostle was sent particularly to his own people, whereas I was sent to every black and red person." [9]

---

[6] Bukhārī.
[7] Qur'ān 34:28.
[8] Qur'ān 21:107.
[9] Muslim.

Amazingly, some Christian Unitarians believe that Muhammad ﷺ was a Prophet, however, they say that he was a Prophet for the Arabs only. Does that mean that he lied when he said, 'I have been sent to the whole of mankind?' If this is the case, then how can a liar be a Prophet? Furthermore, no other Prophet has ever claimed that he was sent to the whole world.

Even Jesus [Sayyidunā Īsā ﷺ] said, 'I have been sent to gather the scattered sheep of the Israelites. [10] Only Muhammad ﷺ claimed to be a universal Prophet. Therefore, when you believe that he was a Prophet of God, then it follows that you will believe him when he says, 'I am a Prophet for all nations and all races.'

"That warn thy people..." Prophets are sent with two messages:

1. Glad tidings.
2. Warnings.

The glad tidings and good news are for those who believe them and follow their call. The warnings are for those who reject them. Since the majority of people are neglectful, are engrossed in worldly pleasures, and refuse to accept the invitation of the Prophets, warnings have been mentioned more often in comparison to glad tidings. In the verse under discussion too, only warning has been mentioned. Warnings are for those whose hearts have become hard like rocks. Glad tidings are for those who wish to purchase the bounties of the hereafter.

However, there are those whose main goal is the pleasure of their Rabb. Their sights are set upon the Creator. If they ask for Jannah, it is because Jannah is the place wherein lies the pleasure of the Rabb Almighty: And if they seek protection from Jahannam, it is because Jahannam is the place wherein lies the anger and wrath of the Rabb.

---

[10] Matthew.

When Khwāja Mawdood Chishtī ﷺ was on his death bed, someone prayed that may Allāh give him Jannah. He opened his eyes and said, 'Are you praying that I get Jannah? Jannah was being presented to me for the last thirty [30] years, but I never gave it a glance. I am in search of the Creator of Jannah.'

"Before a severe chastisement befalls them..." This chastisement came in the form of a huge flood, which wiped out the whole nation from the face of this earth.

VERSE 2

قَالَ يَٰقَوْمِ اِنِّىْ لَكُمْ نَذِيْرٌ مُّبِيْنٌ ﴿٢﴾

"He said: 'O my people.' I am indeed a clear warner to you."

'*Mubeen*' means clear, plain or manifest. The prophets give a very clear message, unlike many of those leaders or philosophers whose language is hard to understand and even more difficult to follow. We also find some gurus who prophesise many events in such an absurd and unclear manner that one may begin to doubt whether the speaker himself realises what he is saying. When a prophet speaks, he speaks very clearly. Ā'ishah ﷺ says:

> 'The Prophet ﷺ would speak in such manner that if a person wanted to count the number of words, he would be able to do so.' [11]

Sometimes he would repeat himself three times so that each person could understand.

---

[11] Bukhārī 3567, Muslim 2493.

VERSE 3

اَنِ اعْبُدُوا اللّٰهَ وَاتَّقُوْهُ وَأَطِيْعُوْنِ ﴿٣﴾

That worship Allāh, fear him, and obey me.

Prophet Nūh ﷺ gave three instructions to his nation:

> 1. Worship Allāh ﷻ alone, and not the idols which you
> have made for yourselves such as: Wadd, Suwaa,
> Yaghoos, and Nasr.

Looking at the Aḥādīth, one can understand that *ibādah* [worship] is
sometimes used for *tawḥīd*, and sometimes for worship. In a Hadith in
Ṣaḥīḥ Muslim, the Prophet ﷺ was asked: 'Tell me, O Rasūlallāh, what
will draw me closer to Jannah and distance me from Jahannam?" The
Prophet liked the question and looked at the saḥāba and said, 'This
man has some understanding!' Then he told the person to repeat the
question, and then replied, 'That you worship Allāh, you do not join
any partners unto him, you take care of salāh, you pay zakāh, and you
join your family ties.' [12]

In the Hadīth of Jibra'īl, the Prophet ﷺ was asked, 'What is Islam?'
He replied, 'Islam is that you worship Allāh, you do not associate any
partners with Him, you establish salāh which has been fixed upon you,
and you pay the zakāh which has been prescribed for you, you fast
[the month of] Ramadhān, and you perform Hajj if it is possible for
you to undertake the journey.' [13]

The commentators have put forward two explanations for the
word 'worship Allāh':

---

[12] Muslim, Vol 1, Pg. 31.
[13] Muslim, 28.

i.   *Tawhīd*, i.e. firm belief in the oneness of Allāh.

ii.   Worshipping Allāh by following his commands.

In the verse under discussion, it seems that the second meaning is taken, i.e. engage yourself in all forms of worship.

2. The second instruction is to fear Allāh. *Taqwā* literally means 'to take care' or 'to protect'. Thereafter, it is used for constant awareness of Allāh ﷻ meaning that one takes care of the orders of Allāh ﷻ in the most careful manner; that is by creating that special bond which makes one realise that he is under the watchful eye of Allāh ﷻ, then one has this fear of His displeasure. When you dearly love someone, you hate to annoy them out of fear that you might lose them. Similarly, one must love Allāh to the extent that one would fear his displeasure, which would urge him to obey Allāh ﷻ, to engage in His *dhikr*, and refrain from all forms of disobedience. This feeling would rise until the level where one could not live without Him, when one is constantly thinking about Him and cannot bear His separation. As a poet says:

خيالُك فِيْ عَيْنِيْ وذِكْرُكَ فِيْ فمِي ومَثْوَاكَ فِيْ قَلْبِيْ فاينَ تَغِيْبُ ـ

'Your thoughts are in my mind, your remembrance is on my lips, and you are staying in my heart, so how can you hide from me.'

3. The third instruction is that 'obey me'. Prophets are sent to be obeyed. Obeying a Prophet is not *shirk* because the prophets duty is to deliver the orders of Allāh ﷻ. So he is sent by Allāh ﷻ to be obeyed. The Qur'ān says:

$$\text{مَّن يُطِعِ الرَّسُوْلَ فَقَدْ اَطَاعَ اللّٰهَ} \ \clubsuit$$

'Whosoever obeys the Prophet has obeyed Allāh.' [14]

Allāh ﷻ says:

$$\text{وَاِنْ تُطِيْعُوْهُ تَهْتَدُوْا} \ \clubsuit$$

'If you obey him, you will be guided.' [15]

He also says:

$$\text{يَاۤ اَيُّهَا الَّذِيْنَ اٰمَنُوْاۤ اَطِيْعُوا اللّٰهَ وَاَطِيْعُوا الرَّسُوْلَ وَاُولِى الْاَمْرِ مِنْكُمْ} \ \clubsuit$$

'O you who believe! Obey Allāh and His Messenger and those
amongst you who have the authority.' [16]

With these verses, one can refute the claims of two different sects:

1. The *Munkireen* of Hadīth, who call themselves the
'*Ahlul Qur'ān*' [People of the Qur'ān]. Their claim is that
we should follow nothing but the Qur'ān. They refuse
to accept the Prophet ﷺ as an authority and put
forward flimsy arguments to support their claim. The
above verses prove that the Qur'ān itself is stating that
whether you like it or not, the Prophet ﷺ should be
obeyed under all circumstances. Ahādīth are the
sayings of the Prophet ﷺ. They are the commentaries
of the Qur'ān, therefore, they have to be taken
seriously.

---

[14] Qur'an 4:80.
[15] Qur'an 24:54.
[16] Qur'an 4:59.

2. The second claim is of those who call themselves *'Ahlul Hadīth'* [People of the Hadīth]. They restrict their obedience to the Hadīth and refuse to pay any attention to the rulings given by the *fuqahā* and *muftiyā-e-kiraam*.

As the first sect deviated by claiming that only the Qur'ān should be followed and not the Hadīth, the second group also deviated by claiming that only the Hadīth should be followed and not any of the Imāms. These people go to the extent of labelling *taqleed* as *shirk*.

One must realise that following a Prophet is not *shirk*, because the Prophet's duty is to convey and explain the order of Allāh ﷻ. Similarly, following an Imām is not *shirk*, because an Imām does not invent the rulings, he only derives rulings from the Qur'ān and Hadīth and explains them to us. Every human does not have the capacity to derive daily *masā'il* from the Qur'ān and Hadīth. One has no choice but to rely on someone who has carefully studied the Qur'ān and Hadīth and has the ability to derive *masā'il* from there. This reliance and trust is known as *taqleed*.

Let me explain this by stating my own experience. I am a *Hanafī* scholar and proud to be so. *Alhamdulillāh*, the *Hanafī* school of *Fiqh* is the most comprehensive school. Throughout the fourteen [14] centuries that have passed, we see that the *fuqahā* of *ahnāf* have sacrificed their lives to engaging in extensive research. They have prepared books for us which consist of the *usool* of sharī'ah and the *furū'* of sharī'ah [i.e. the roots and branches of the day to day *masā'il*]. The muftī's job is to first study the Arabic language and then the Qur'ān and Ahādīth, and then he has to undergo a course of studies in which he has to learn the rules of *fatwā*. Next, he has to achieve expertise in finding the *masā'il* from their appropriate places. I myself have studied *Iftā*, although I am reluctant in giving *fatwās*.

Once a young girl sent in a question: 'If a girl has been raped and she became pregnant, can she have an abortion?' I couldn't answer immediately so I promised to investigate and reply as quickly as possible. Now one must realise that he can never find the answer to this question directly in any verse of the Qur'ān nor in any Ahādīth. I challenge the whole *salafī* world to find me the answer in the Qur'ān or in the Hadīth. One has to refer to an *Ālim*. I phoned my teacher Hadhrat Muftī Shabbīr Sāhib and consulted him.

The answer is that the girl is at no fault in the tragedy that befell her. Once a similar case was brought to the Prophet ﷺ. He said to the woman, 'Go! Allāh has forgiven you.' Then he ordered that the penalty be carried out upon the accused. [17]

Although the case in this Hadīth is similar to our question, however, with regards to abortion, it must be noted, that this cannot be traced back to the era of the Prophet ﷺ. They did not have the tools and therefore they could not have contemplated abortion. Therefore such a question and answer cannot be found in Hadīth.

Now pondering over the rules laid out by jurists in the light of the Qur'ān and Ahādīth, we can deduce that abortion would either be sought after the *rooh* [soul] has been breathed into the foetus, or before that. In the first condition, it will not be allowed under any circumstance, because it will be the cause of killing a living person, and that is *harām* in Islam. Therefore, once the *rooh* has entered the body, abortion is out of the question.

However, in the second condition, i.e. when the *rooh* has not entered the body, [which takes place after four months into the pregnancy], then it could be allowed under certain circumstances, e.g. when the life of the mother is in danger. Each individual will have to put her case before a Muftī, who can look at her situation and give her a ruling accordingly. In our case, it would not be good for the girl to have an abortion. It is better for her to keep the child. However, if she is under enormous pressure, that in this state no one will marry her,

---

[17] Tirmidhī, Abū Dāwūd, Mishkāt Pg. 312.

or she will have a bad name in the community, she could be permitted to abort the foetus as long as the soul has not entered the body.

I have drifted away from my original point. I would like to say that the *salafis* have only come into existence in the past century. If one delves a bit further, one can ascertain that all the great *Ulamā*, commentators of Hadīth and *tasfīr* were followers of a particular school of *Fiqh*. Ibn Hajar Asqalānī, Badruddin Aynī, Qādhī Iyāz Mālikī, Ibn Qudāmā Hanbalī, Ibn Kathīr, Qurtubī, Imām Nawawī, Imām Bayhaqī, Imām Tahāwī, Ibn Taymīyah, Ibn Qayyim, Ibn Rajab, and most of the *Musannifeen* of the *al-Sihah al-Sittah*, and the list goes on and on; all of them followed a *madhab* [a school of thought]. They found it safer to do so and better than following one's own desire by choosing from the vast collection of Ahādīth. Therefore, I urge the reader to stick to a *madhab*, whether *Hanafī*, *Mālikī*, *Shāfi'ī*, or *Hanbalī*, because in doing so, we are treading the path of our rightly guided *Ulamā*. May Allāh ﷻ keep us steadfast upon the straight path. Āmīn!

VERSE 4

يَغْفِرْ لَكُمْ مِّنْ ذُنُوْبِكُمْ وَيُؤَخِّرْكُمْ اِلٰى اَجَلٍ مُّسَمًّى ط

اِنَّ اَجَلَ اللهِ اِذَا جَآءَ لَا يُؤَخَّرُ ۘ لَوْ كُنْتُمْ تَعْلَمُوْنَ ﴿٤﴾

"So that He may forgive you some of your sins and give you respite for a
stated term; for when the term given by Allāh is accomplished, it cannot be
differed, if ye only knew."

Sayyidunā Nūh ﷺ is saying that if you worship Allāh ﷻ, fear Him, and obey Him, then Allāh ﷻ will gift you with two favours:

1. He will forgive you some of your sins.
2. He will give you respite.

Khāzin 🕮 says, 'By some sins, He means those which were committed up to believing in Sayyidunā Nūh 🕮. There is no guarantee of the sins that would be committed after that.'

Nasafī 🕮 states, 'Those sins which are related to other people cannot be forgiven, and properties have to be returned to their rightful owners, e.g. stolen goods, items bought but not paid for, amānats which need to be returned, debts which need to be paid off etc.

In a Hadīth in *Sahīh Muslim*, the Prophet 🕮 says: 'Islam annihilates all the sins which were committed before it.'

Shaykh Mūsā Shāheen Al-Misrī writes in the commentary that there is some detailed explanation here. The non-believer who embraces Islam will fall into one of two categories. He was either a) *Harbī* or b) *Zimmi*. [18]

If a *Harbī kāfir* was to become a Muslim, all his sins will be abolished, whether they are related to Allāh or to human beings. Therefore, *Qisās* cannot be taken from him. He will not be held responsible if he had destroyed some property of a Muslim prior to his entrance into the fold of Islam. If he had committed *zinā* [fornication] and then he embraced Islam, then the punishment of *zinā* will not be inflicted upon him. However, if he had seized a Muslim's belongings beforehand, then there is a difference of opinion as to whether he should be held responsible for returning those goods to the Muslim:

1. Imām Mālik 🕮 says, 'They will remain his property.'

2. Imām Shāfi'ī 🕮 says, 'He will have to return to the rightful owner all those goods that are still under his

---

[18] *Harbī*: Living in *Dārul Harb*, *Zimmī*: Living in *Dārul Islam* under the protection of Muslims.

possession, because he is likened to the usurper, who takes illegal possession.'

The *Hanafi maslak* seems to be the same as the *Shāfi'ī madhab*. Allāmā Shabbir Ahmed Uthmānī ﷾ writes, '. . . If he had taken something as a loan or brought some goods but not paid for them yet, then he will be responsible even after embracing Islam.'

If he were a *Zimmī kāfir* then his Islam will not abort his liabilities. He will have to return whatever he had taken illegally, and he will be held accountable for any injuries he had inflicted upon someone or any murder or crime he had committed. This is because the rules of Islam had applied to him [i.e. while staying in *Dārul Islam*, he was required to abide by the rules of Islam]. Allāmā Uthmānī ﷾ says, 'There is a consensus of the ulamā upon this.' [19]

Once during the month of Ramadhān, a *tablīghī jamā'at* from the USA came to our local masjid. Among them was a revert. He used to listen to my discourses very attentively, even though they were in Urdu and he could not understand Urdu. He befriended me and showered me with questions. One of his questions was, whether he was liable for whatever he had taken from people before embracing Islam. At the time I could not recall the answer. So after consulting our Muftī Sāhib, I told him that he must repay whatever he could because he was not in *Dārul Islam*, but neither was he in *Dārul Harb*. He was somewhere in between. So it was better to be cautious and repay as much as possible. The same would be the case for those brothers and sisters who embrace Islam here in the UK. They should try and clear their accounts and repay whatever they can to their creditors.

May Allāh ﷻ give us the *tawfeeq* to practice upon His *deen* in the correct manner. Āmīn!

He also asked me another question. He said that I was told that it is okay to do *masah* on thin cotton socks. I used to do that but now I

---

[19] Fathul Mun'im, Vol. 2, Pg. 112; Fathul Mul'him, Vol. 1, Pg. 272.

have come to know that this is wrong. Should I do *qadhā* of the *salāh* which I have prayed in the last five years?

Let me just elaborate on this *mas'ala*. When Allāh ﷻ gives the order of *wudhū* in Sūrah Mā'idah [20], He commands us to wash three limbs [the arms, the face and the feet], and to pass wet hands over one, the head. Therefore, the *wazeefah* [duty] of the feet is washing. Now the Qur'ān is *nass qat'ee*. To move from this firm order, we need something as firm as the verse of the Qur'ān.

Therefore, when we study the books of Ahādīth, we see that *masah* over *khuffain* [leather socks] has been mentioned in the *mutawātir* Ahādīth, which are as firm and strong as the Qur'ānic verse. Hence, adding this *mas'ala* to the Qur'ān is allowed.

Therefore, when the feet are open, they have to be washed [only the *Rawaafidh*, Shia believe that the feet will be wiped just as the head], and when they are covered with leather socks they will be wiped over as mentioned in the *Sahīh* Ahādīth of *Sahīh al-Bukhārī*, *Sahīh Muslim*, and others. Imām Hassan Basrī ﷺ says, 'Masah alal khuffain' has been narrated by more than 70 *Sahābā*. Imām Abū Hanīfā ﷺ says, 'I did not take the opinion of "masah alal khuffain" until so many Ahādīth came which were like the daylight.'

Now when we come to the *mas'ala* of *masah* on cotton socks, we see that there is no Hadīth for 'masah alal jawrab' in *Sahīh al-Bukhārī* or in *Sahīh Muslim*. [N.B. Many *Salafis* narrate the Hadīth of *Sahīh al-Bukhārī* regarding *masah* on *khuff* and translate *khuff* as socks. This is misleading because *khuff* is a word which is exclusively used for leather socks. Cotton socks are called *jawrab*. There is a Hadīth of this type [*masah* on the cotton socks] in Sunan al-Tirmīdhī and Sunan Abū Dāwūd which is *dhaeef*, weak.

Imām Abū Dāwūd has declared this Hadīth as *dhaeef*, and so too have Yahyā ibn Maeen, Abdul Rahmān ibn Mahdī, and Alī ibn Al Madīnī. The reason being is that there are two narrators in this Hadīth

---

[20] Qur'ān 5:6.

who are *dhaeef*: [1] Abū Qays Al Awadi, and, [2] Huzail ibn Shurahbeel.
[21]

Imām Abū Dāwūd narrated this Hadīth and said: 'And Abdul Rahmān ibn Mahdī would not narrate this Hadīth because what is famous from Mughīra is that the Prophet ﷺ wiped over *khuffain* [Leather socks].' [22]

So how can people who always question our evidences and reject them by saying '*Dhaeef*! *Dhaeef*!' hang on to such a *dhaeef* Hadīth? They should provide a Sahīh Hadīth from either *Sahīh al-Bukhārī* or *Sahīh Muslim*.

Those Imāms who have allowed *masah alal-jawrab* have restricted this permission with 'thick socks', which do not let water seep through and in which it would be possible to walk a long distance while wearing the socks only. The same has been narrated from the *Hanafī* school, [see *Shāmī*] *Shāfi'ī* school [*Al-Majmoo'* of Imām Nawawī], and *Hanbalī* school [al Mughnī of ibn Qudāmā].

So if someone purchased socks which are made from waterproof material, and which are thick enough that it is possible to walk in them without any other footwear, as is possible with *khuffain*, then it would be permissible to do *masah* over them as they are closer to *khuffain*. However, these thin cotton socks we wear, we are not allowed to do *masah* over them under any circumstances.

Coming back to the original question, I had to consult Muftī Shabbir Sāhib and then gave him the reply that he will not have to do Qadhā for his previous *salāh* due to the fact that he had asked a scholar and acted upon his advice, therefore, he will not be held responsible, and will not have to do *Qadhā*. However, since he has now known the correct *mas'ala*, he must refrain from this in future.

I have seen people standing in a pool of water in the *wudhū khānā* where they did *wudhū*. They made *masah* on top while their cotton

---

[21] Darse Tirmidhī, Vol. 1, Pg. 336. Tirmidhī 122, Abu Dāwūd, Pg. 24.
[22] Abu Dāwūd Pg. 24.

socks were drenched in water from beneath, and then entered the masjid wetting the whole carpet as they walked to the front.

Once at Manchester airport prayer room, I saw a person who had done *masah* on his big Dr. Marten shoes. He came to the prayer room, undid his shoe laces, took the shoes off and started his *salāh*. His *masah* was left on his shoes.

One teacher in Islāmīyyah School in London had become a *salafiyyā*. After some time, she returned to the *Hanafī maslak* saying that these people play with the *deen*. They told us to do *masah* on socks, then told us to do *masah* on our headgear as well. What kind of *deen* is this? She said it is better to stick to a *madhab* where we get clear guidelines from authentic scholars.

Finally, we should realise that we are dealing with the matter of *salāh*. We should take great care and try to perform *salāh* in a manner that is correct according to all the *madhāhib*.

Also, if we had to face a little bit of difficulty in taking our socks off, we should not hesitate. The Hadīth says, 'Shall I not tell you deeds by which Allāh wipes out sins and raises ranks? Completing *wudhū* in spite of disliking it, frequenting steps towards masājid, and waiting for *salāh* after *salāh*.' [23]

Another Hadīth says: 'Nothing is more beloved to Allāh than two drops and two marks. Drops of tears due to fear of Allāh, and a drop of blood shed in the path of Allāh. As for the two marks, one is a scar received in the path of Allāh and the other is the result and aftermath of an obligation from obligatory deeds fixed by Allāh.'[24] The commentators say that this means the splitting and cracking of the feet and hands due to performing wudhū with cold water.

May Allāh ﷻ give us the correct understanding of *deen* and the *tawfeeq* to practice upon it. Āmīn!

---

[23] Muslim.

[24] Tirmidhī, Mishkāt 333.

The second favour of Allāh ﷻ would be the respite given to them up to a stated term. Khāzin says: 'This means that up to the time of your natural death, and therefore He will not punish you.' Nasafī also states that the stated term is the time of their death.

Ibn Kathīr ﷺ narrated here that some commentators use this verse as their evidence to prove that some deeds can increase the lifespan, as a Hadīth says:

إِنَّ صِلَةَ الرَّحِمِ مَحَبَّةٌ فِي الأَهْلِ مَثْرَاةٌ فِي المَالِ مَنْسَأَةٌ فِي الأَثَرِ .

'For indeed keeping the ties of kinship encourages affection among the relatives, increases the wealth, and increases the lifespan.' [25]

Muftī Shafī Sāhib ﷺ explains this further in his *Mā'riful Qur'ān*. He narrates from *Tasfīr Mazharī* that *taqdeer* [fate] is of two types:

1. *Mubram*: irrevocable, absolute, definite.

2. *Muallaq*: Pending, conditioned. This means that in the *Lawh-e-mahfooz* [the Sacred Tablet], it is written that if such and such a person performs a certain deed, his lifespan will be increased by up to seventy [70] years for example. However, if he does not perform it, he will only live for sixty [60] years. Additionally, from the negative side, if he were to commit this act, his life would be reduced to fifty years, and otherwise he would be given respite for up to sixty [60] years. Both types of *taqdeer* are mentioned in the Qur'ān. Allāh ﷻ says:

يَمْحُو اللهُ مَا يَشَاءُ وَيُثْبِتُ ۖ وَعِنْدَهُ أُمُّ الْكِتَبِ ۞

'Allāh does blot out what He pleases or confirms it,

---

[25] Tirmidhī.

and with Him is the Mother of the Book.' [26]

However, this second *taqdeer* is in relation to us and in relation to the angels who note down that *taqdeer*. Allāh ﷻ himself knows the final outcome with certainty, and that is why He blots out and confirms what He wishes.

The Hadīth of Salmān Fārsī ﷺ, narrated by Imām Tirmīdhī, states that the Prophet ﷺ said:

$$ \text{لا يَرُدُّ القَضَاءَ الاَّ الدُّعَاءُ ـ ولا يَزِيدُ فِي العُمرِ الَّا البِرُّ .} $$

'Nothing besides duā can reverse the taqdeer, and nothing
other than servitude to parents can increase the lifespan.'

The conclusion is that in this portion of the *ayah*, Allāh ﷻ is referring to the *taqdeer-e-muallaq*, which means that if they were to believe in Prophet Nūh ﷺ, they would be given respite to live up to the stated term, which Allāh ﷻ has originally destined for them, and they would not be wiped out from the face of the earth by any form of punishment. On the other hand, if they rejected Nūh ﷺ, then the punishment would descend upon them in this world and the chastisement of the hereafter would be added to that.

Thereafter, Sayyidunā Nūh ﷺ speaks of the *taqdeer-e-mubram*, that when the time fixed by Allāh ﷻ draws closer, nothing can delay it. Each person will die on the time that has been fixed for him/her. No one will live in this world forever and ever. Allāh ﷻ has created the routine of this world in such a way that each and every person has to die upon their fixed time.

Allāmā Shabbīr Ahmed Uthmānī ﷺ writes: 'If you come to believe then God will forgive you for your previous violations of divine obligations. The chastisement destined to come in case of disbelief and insolence, will not come, and this will be due to the blessings of

---

[26] Qur'ān 13:39.

Īmān. You shall be given respite to live up to your natural age under the general law of life and death, and this is inevitable for every good and bad soul in this world. However, if the promise of chastisement hovers above your heads in the case that you do not worship, it would not be averted by anyone, nor would respite of a single minute be given.'

Hadhrat Shah Abdul Qādir Dehlavī Sāhib says: 'O people! Worship so that mankind may survive in the world until the day of *Qiyāmah*, and the day of *Qiyāmah* will not be delayed. And if you abandon worship altogether, then you shall be finished there and then altogether. The Great Flood came in such a manner that no one would have survived, but mankind were saved by the faith and obedience of Sayyidunā Nūh ﷺ and his companions.' [27]

Some commentators say that increasing lifespan is by increasing the ability to worship Allāh ﷻ. Some do so much good in a 50 year life which others can't do in 80 years of life. This Barakah in life comes with obedience to parents, elders, teachers and mashāikh.

"...If ye only knew...' Allāmā Uthmānī ﷺ writes: 'If you possess understanding, then these things should be understood and acted upon.'

VERSES 5–6

$$\text{قَالَ رَبِّ اِنِّىْ دَعَوْتُ قَوْمِىْ لَيْلًا وَّنَهَارًا ﴿٥﴾}$$

$$\text{فَلَمْ يَزِدْهُمْ دُعَآءِىْ اِلَّا فِرَارًا ﴿٦﴾}$$

He said: "O my Rabb! Verily I have called my people by night and day."
But my invitation only increased them in flight [from the right].

---

[27] Tafsīr Uthmānī, Pg.2454.

Allāmā Shabbīr Ahmed Uthmānī ﷺ writes: 'It means that Sayyidunā Nūh ﷺ had been preaching to them for nine hundred and fifty [950] years. But when he saw no ray of hope, he pleaded to his Rabb in utter disgust and disappointment.' He said: 'My Rabb! I left no stone unturned in delivering Thy message to them, I went on calling them unto Thee in the darkness of night and in broad daylight, but the result was that the more I called them, the more they ran away from me; and the greater the kindness and the prophetic love was shown from me, the greater their aversion and hatred increased against me.'

Abdullāh Yūsuf Alī writes, 'When convincing arguments and warnings are put before sinners, there are two kinds of reactions. Those who are wise receive admonition, repent, and bring forth the fruits of repentance, i.e. amend their lives and turn to Allāh - on the other hand, those who are callous to any advice, take it up as a reproach, fly farther and farther from righteousness and shut out more and more of the channels through which Allāh's healing grace can reach them and work for them.'

Nasafī narrates here that a person would take his son to Sayyidunā Nūh ﷺ and, pointing towards him, he would say, 'Stay well clear of this man. Do not let him deceive you. My father also gave me strict advice in this regard.'

Muftī Shafī Sāhib ﷺ writes in *Ma'riful Qur'ān* that the lifespan of the people of Nūh ﷺ was not as long as that of himself. Nūh's ﷺ life of nearly a thousand years was also of a miraculous nature. Nūh ﷺ outlived two to three generations of his own *Ummah*.

Calling towards Allāh ﷻ has been the duty of the messengers of Allāh ﷻ. They fulfilled this duty to the best of their ability. It had begun from the time of Nūh ﷺ. Thereafter, every prophet called towards Allāh ﷻ, until the final Prophet Muhammad Mustafā ﷺ came to this world. He also performed the work of *Da'wah* and *tablīgh* [calling and reaching out to people]. Allāh ﷻ says:

$$\text{قُلْ هٰذِهٖ سَبِيْلِيْ اَدْعُوْٓا اِلَى اللهِ قف عَلٰى بَصِيْرَةٍ اَنَا وَمَنِ اتَّبَعَنِيْ ۝}$$

"Say [O Muhammad] this is my path. I call [people]
to Allāh with full insight – myself and my followers." [28]

The Prophet ﷺ was given clear guidelines with regards to the work of
Da'wah. In Sūrah Nahl, we read:

$$\text{اُدْعُ اِلٰى سَبِيْلِ رَبِّكَ بِالْحِكْمَةِ وَالْمَوْعِظَةِ الْحَسَنَةِ ۝}$$

"Invite people to the way of your Rabb with wisdom and good counsel." [29]

One of the titles he was given is 'Al-Da'ee'. Allāh ﷻ says:

$$\text{وَدَاعِيًا اِلَى اللهِ بِاِذْنِهٖ وَسِرَاجًا مُّنِيْرًا ۝}$$

"[And we have sent you as an] … inviter to Allāh by his commands and as
an illuminating lamp." [30]

The Qur'ān says:

$$\text{يٰقَوْمَنَآ اَجِيْبُوْا دَاعِيَ اللهِ ۝}$$

"O our people! Respond to the caller of Allāh [Prophet Muhammad ﷺ]." [31]

This duty has now been passed on to his *Ummah*. Therefore, we are
also *dāees* [callers to Allāh]. And we should always bear in mind the
guidance given to the Prophet ﷺ in Sūrah al-Nahl. If we ponder over
that verse, we learn four important aspects of *hidāyah* [guidance]:

---

[28] Qur'ān 12:108.
[29] Qur'ān 16:125.
[30] Qur'ān 33:46.
[31] Qur'ān 46:31.

1. اِدْعُ The very first words used are 'Da'wah' [invitation]. If you wanted to invite someone to an important function, how would you go about it? Would you shout at the person, curse him, accuse him? – Or would you speak in a soft tone? Ask him nicely; write a nice appealing invitation card so that he might be inclined towards accepting your invitation? Of course you would choose the second option to be successful in getting him to your desired place. Similar is the case of inviting towards the deen. The first rule is that you talk in a soft, appealing, gentle, and kind manner.

Alhamdulillāh, today we see that when the *tablīghī jamā'at* go out for the work of *Da'wah*, they adopt this manner and speak to the addressee in the softest possible tone. May Allāh 🕮 reward them and accept their efforts. Āmīn!

2. سَبِيلِ رَبِّكَ 'The path of your Rabb'. This indicates the fact that the call should not be towards one's self, or towards one's own ideology. Rather, the caller should show the utmost sincerity by bearing in mind that his mission is to call people to Allāh 🕮. Therefore, if the addressee just turns up at the masjid for *salāh*, then he is successful.

3. بِالْحِكْمَةِ 'With wisdom'. Let us go a bit deeper into the meaning of 'Bil Hikmah'.

Tasfīr Rūhul-Ma'ānī narrates from *Al-Bahrul-Muhīt*: 'It is a sound speech which goes to the depth of the heart in the most beautiful manner.'
    '*Rūhul-Bayān*' states:

Al-*Hikmah* means the insight through which one finds out the dictates of circumstances and talks as relatively appropriate, chooses such time and occasion as would not put burden on the addressee, employs lenience where lenience is called for, and firmness where firmness is in order. And where he thinks the addressee would be embarrassed by saying something frankly, he should communicate subtly [and avoid embarrassing the person]. [32]

Therefore, when we call someone to Allāh ﷻ, we should adopt the most suitable manner, use words of wisdom, and narrate some nice stories of our pious predecessors in order to bring the person closer to Allāh ﷻ.

4. الموعظة الحسنة . "وعظ" means to say something in the spirit of wishing well in a manner that would make the heart of the addressee softened, and turned in to accepting what he is about to receive.

Once the Prophet ﷺ talked to a person and invited him towards Islam. The person asked: 'Why should I believe in you? Is there any reason why I should leave my gods and my religion? The Prophet ﷺ replied [to the effect]: 'Tell me, if you were travelling through a desert or a jungle, and you were separated from your caravan, and you lost your way. [And] Now you are surrounded by beasts and reptiles. You don't know which step will lead you to your death. Suddenly a man appears in front of you. You know that person, he is from your tribe. He says come! I know the way out of here; I will lead you to safety. Will you follow him or not? He said, 'Of course I will follow him.' The Prophet ﷺ said, 'Well, I am trying to guide you out of a much worse situation

---

[32] Mā'riful Qur'ān, Vol.5, Pg.43.

and taking you to safety [i.e. from the punishment of *Jahannam* to the security of *Jannah*].' The person embraced Islam. Thereafter, he used to say I met someone with whom there was no room for argument. I had to accept what he said. [33]

Once he invited Rukanah, the champion wrestler of Makkah Mukarramah. Rukanah said if you beat me in wrestling, I will believe you. The Prophet ﷺ agreed. They wrestled and he pinned Rukanah down. Rukanah was stunned. He refused to accept defeat and asked for a second bout. He beat him again. And then for a third time as well. Now Rukanah had no choice. He could not understand how an average person like Rasūlullāh ﷺ could defeat a heavy weight wrestler. He embraced Islam and went on to be one of the great Sahābā - I am not saying all readers should start wrestling in order to propagate Islam, but the moral is that we should adopt any suitable manner and we must leave no stone unturned, nor let go of any opportunity when calling to Allāh ﷻ.

Alhamdulillāh, the *Tablīghī Jamā'at* is doing an excellent job. They need our support and we should provide that and participate however we can in the work of *Dā'wah*.

There are other ways of dā'wah as well. Many organisations reach out to non-Muslims. We should help them as much as we can. Īmām Sirāj Wahhāj of New York says that Muslims are way behind in this. We, as Christians, used to attend college during weekdays and then over the weekend, we would stand in the cold and rain in the centre of the city. We would talk to people and distribute leaflets throughout the whole day. Muslims needs to organise such events too.

VERSE 7

وَاِنِّىْ كُلَّمَا دَعَوْتُهُمْ لِتَغْفِرَ لَهُمْ جَعَلُوْٓا اَصَابِعَهُمْ فِىْ اٰذَانِهِمْ

---

[33] Tafsīr Ibn Kathīr.

$$\text{وَاسْتَغْشَوْا ثِيَابَهُمْ وَأَصَرُّوا وَاسْتَكْبَرُوا اسْتِكْبَارًا ﴿٧﴾}$$

And every time I called them so that Thou may forgive them, they only
turned away, thrust their fingers into their ears, covered themselves up with
their garments, and they persisted and showed pride, a great pride.

"They thrust their fingers into their ears..." Because they could not
tolerate to hear me, they used their fingers to stop my voice from
going into their ears. They wrapped themselves in their garments and
changed their appearance so that I would not recognize them.
Moreover, if their fingers became loose, then their clothes might help
in covering their ears. By any means, they did not want my words to
enter their ears.

"They persisted..." They did not desire to move from their way and their
pride did not allow them to pay the slightest attention to my call.

"And they showed pride..." The common diseases among the nations of
the past were *kufr* and *shirk*. However on top of that, each nation had
some specific ailment. For example, the nation of Hūd ﷺ had
'takabbur' [pride and haughtiness]. The nation of Sālih ﷺ were
engrossed in gaining worldly pleasure through orchards and gardens
and were the most ungrateful people. The people of Lūt ﷺ initiated
homosexuality. The people of Nūh ﷺ were proud people. Allāh ﷻ says
in Sūrah al-Zāriyāt:

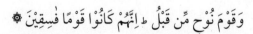

"[We have destroyed] the Nation of Nūh beforehand.
Indeed they were a nation of Transgressors." [34]

---

[34] Qur'ān 51:46.

Their pride stems from their words, which they said to Nūh ﷺ:

$$\text{قَالُوٓا اَنُؤۡمِنُ لَكَ وَاتَّبَعَكَ الۡاَرۡذَلُوۡنَ ۝}$$

'Should we believe in you when the lowest of the lowly
people have followed you?' [35]

They also said to Nūh ﷺ and his followers:

$$\text{مَا نَرٰىكَ اِلَّا بَشَرًا مِّثۡلَنَا وَمَا نَرٰىكَ اتَّبَعَكَ اِلَّا الَّذِيۡنَ هُمۡ اَرَاذِلُنَا بَادِىَ}$$

$$\text{الرَّاۡىِ ۚ وَمَا نَرٰى لَكُمۡ عَلَيۡنَا مِنۡ فَضۡلٍ ۢ بَلۡ نَظُنُّكُمۡ كٰذِبِيۡنَ ۝}$$

'We see [in] you nothing but a man like ourselves and we see that only
those people follow you who are of low class and who are simple minded.
Nor do we see in you [all] any merit above us; in fact we think that you are
liars.' [36]

In Sūrah Al-Najm, Allāh ﷻ says:

$$\text{وَقَوۡمَ نُوۡحٍ مِّنۡ قَبۡلُ ؕ اِنَّهُمۡ كَانُوۡا هُمۡ اَظۡلَمَ وَاَطۡغٰى ۝}$$

'And before them, the people of Nūh, for they were
[all] most unjust and most insolent Transgressors.' [37]

There are many diseases which kill off the soul. 'Takabbur' is the most
harmful of them all. The *sūfiyā kirām* regard it as the most dangerous.

Hadhrat Shaykh-al-Hadīth Imām Muhammad Zakariyyā ﷺ had a
special book written on this subject. It is called ام الامراض [*Ummul
Amrādh - The Mother of all Ailments*].

Here are a few excerpts from the book:

---

[35] Qur'ān 26:111.

[36] Qur'ān 11:27.

[37] Qur'ān 53:52.

Allāh ﷻ says in the Glorious Qur'ān:

$$\text{سَاَصْرِفُ عَنْ اٰیٰتِیَ الَّذِیْنَ یَتَکَبَّرُوْنَ فِی الْاَرْضِ بِغَیْرِ الْحَقِّ ۞}$$

'I shall turn away from My signs those who show
pride on the earth, when they have no right to do so.' [38]

He also says:

$$\text{اِنَّهٗ لَا یُحِبُّ الْمُسْتَکْبِرِیْنَ ۞}$$

'He does not like the proud people.' [39]

A Hadīth in *Sahīh Muslim* says, 'That person will not enter paradise
who holds pride in his heart equivalent to the weight of an atom.' In
another Hadīth, the Prophet ﷺ says, 'On the day of Judgement, a neck
will appear from inside the fire of Hell. It will have two ears with
which it will hear, two eyes with which it will see, and a tongue with
which it will speak. It will proclaim, 'I have been ordered to seize three
types of people: [1] every proud, stubborn, and arrogant person; [2]
anyone who associated partners with Allāh; [3] and a person who used
to make pictures.'

Another Hadīth says that when Nūh ﷺ was breathing his last, he
called his sons and gave them some advice. He told them to refrain
from *shirk* and *kibr* [arrogance].

Abu Huraira ﷺ narrates that the Prophet ﷺ said, 'The haughty
people shall be resurrected on the day of judgement in the size of ants.
People will be treading over them.'

In another Hadīth, the Prophet ﷺ says, 'Allāh does not even look
at a person who drags his garments on the ground due to pride.'

---

[38] Qur'ān 7:146.
[39] Qur'ān 16:23.

Mutarrif Ibn Abdillah saw Muhallab in silky clothes showing off and walking with pride. Mutarrif said, 'O servant of Allāh! Allāh does not like this manner of walking.' Muhallab said, 'Do you know who I am?' [He was the ruler]. Mutarrif replied, 'Yes I do know who you are. Your beginning is a dirty drop of semen, your ending is a stinking corpse, and in between, you carry filth in your stomach wherever you go.'

Furthermore, *takabbur* [showing pride] leads to *kufr*. In fact, the majority of disbelievers refuse to believe because of *takabbur*. Iblīs refused to prostrate in front of Ādam ﷺ because of his pride:

$$\text{اَبٰى وَاسْتَكْبَرَ ۚ وَكَانَ مِنَ الْكٰفِرِيْنَ} ۝$$

'He refused and was haughty, and he was of those who rejected.'[40]

One Hadīth defines *takabbur* as thus:

$$\text{الْكِبْرُ بَطَرُ الْحَقِّ وغَمْطُ الناس ـ}$$

Kibr is to reject the truth and to degrade people [hold them in contempt].[41]

Another Hadīth says:

'Whosoever makes himself humble for the sake of Allāh, Allāh will raise him. And whosoever shows pride, Allāh will lower his value [bring him down].[42]

May Allāh ﷻ save us from the evil of takabbur. Āmīn

---

[40] Qur'ān 2:34.
[41] Muslim.
[42] Ibn Mājah.

ثُمَّ اِنِّىْ دَعَوْتُهُمْ جِهَارًا ﴿٨﴾ ثُمَّ اِنِّىْ اَعْلَنْتُ لَهُمْ وَاَسْرَرْتُ لَهُمْ اِسْرَارًا

﴿٩﴾ فَقُلْتُ اسْتَغْفِرُوْا رَبَّكُمْ ط اِنَّهُ كَانَ غَفَّارًا ﴿١٠﴾ يُرْسِلِ السَّمَآءَ

عَلَيْكُمْ مِّدْرَارًا ﴿١١﴾ وَيُمْدِدْكُمْ بِاَمْوَالٍ وَّبَنِيْنَ وَيَجْعَلْ لَّكُمْ جَنّٰتٍ

وَّيَجْعَلْ لَّكُمْ اَنْهٰرًا ﴿١٢﴾

Then I called to them aloud. Further, I spoke to them in public and secretly in private. I said: 'Seek forgiveness from your Rabb, for He is forgiving. He will let loose the sky for you in plenteous rain. And will give you increase in wealth and sons; and bestow on you gardens and bestow on you rivers [of flowing water].

The meaning of these next five verses is really clear. Prophet Nūḥ 🙏 is pleading to his Rabb Almighty saying, 'O Allāh! I addressed my nation in their gatherings and in their meeting points. I also took individuals in my confidence and spoke to them in private.' In short Nūḥ 🙏 used all the resources of an earnest preacher but to no avail.

"I said: Seek forgiveness..." Khāzin narrates here that when the people of Nūḥ 🙏 rejected him for a very long period, Allāh 🙏 sent drought and famine upon them. He blocked the rainfall and made the wombs of womenfolk barren for a period of forty [40] years. Their wealth began to perish and their cattle started to die. This is why Nūḥ 🙏 invited them by way of awakening their desires. However, when they still refused to listen, only then did he take a much stricter line with them, warning them of the wrath of Allāh 🙏 if they persisted in their loathsome action.

Nūḥ 🙏 first advised them to seek forgiveness from Allāh 🙏. Nasafī 🙏 writes here that: 'If the person seeking forgiveness is a *kāfir* [non-believer], then his seeking will be for forgiveness of his previous *kufr* [disbelief] by way of believing. And if the seeking person is a sinful believer, then his seeking will be for forgiveness of his past sins [major and minor].'

It is narrated from Umar Ibn Khattāb ﷺ that at a time of drought, he emerged out towards the open fields for *Istisqā* [supplicating for rainfall]. He did nothing more than *Istighfaar*. He sought forgiveness from Allāh continuously and then returned. Someone questioned him that, 'You never said a word about rain.' He replied, 'I have supplicated in the most rightful manner.' Thereafter, he recited these verses of Sūrah Nūh.

Someone approached Hassan Basrī ﷺ and complained to him about his suffering from drought. He prescribed abundance of *Istighfaar* to the person. Another person complained about poverty, he prescribed the same medication. A third person complained about the deficiency of his offspring, he gave the same reply. A fourth person complained about the lack of harvest in his fields, he said the same thing, i.e. abundance of *Istighfaar*. His student Rabee' Ibn Sabeeh enquired as to why he had given the same answer to four different queries. Hasan Basrī ﷺ recited the above verses.

Allāmā Uthmānī ﷺ writes: 'By the blessing of *Īmān* and *Istighfaar*, the drought and famine [in which they were lying for so long] will go away. And Allāh will send rainfall in torrents from the heaven, whereby the fields and gardens shall fructify and become productive of agricultural and horticultural wealth. The animals will regain weight and their milk will increase. The women, who were becoming sterile and barren, due to the misfortune of this disbelief and sinfulness, will become fertile and give birth to male children. In short, along with the wealth of the hereafter, and good fortune of this world will also be given to them.

Note: Imām Abū Hanīfā ﷺ has derived from the indication of the current verses that the essence of *Istisqā* is *Istighfaar* and repentance. However, Sāhibayn say that the most complete form of *Istighfaar* is in 'salāh', so two rak'ahs salāh are also prescribed as narrated in some Ahādīth.

Abdullāh Yūsuf Alī writes: 'If they [the people of Nūh] had taken the message in the right way, the rain would have been a blessing to them. They took it in the wrong way and the rain that came was a curse for them, for it flooded the country and drowned the wicked generation. In the larger plan, it was a blessing all the same, for it purged and gave it a new start, morally and spiritually.' [43]

SOME VIRTUES OF ISTIGHFAAR

Allāh ﷻ says:

وَسَارِعُوْا اِلٰى مَغْفِرَةٍ مِّنْ رَّبِّكُمْ وَجَنَّةٍ عَرْضُهَا السَّمٰوٰتُ وَالْاَرْضُ ۙ اُعِدَّتْ لِلْمُتَّقِيْنَ ۞ الَّذِيْنَ يُنْفِقُوْنَ فِى السَّرَّاءِ وَالضَّرَّاءِ وَالْكٰظِمِيْنَ الْغَيْظَ وَالْعَافِيْنَ عَنِ النَّاسِ ۗ وَاللهُ يُحِبُّ الْمُحْسِنِيْنَ ۞ وَالَّذِيْنَ اِذَا فَعَلُوْا فَاحِشَةً اَوْ ظَلَمُوْا اَنْفُسَهُمْ ذَكَرُوا اللهَ فَاسْتَغْفَرُوْا لِذُنُوْبِهِمْ ص وَمَنْ يَّغْفِرُ الذُّنُوْبَ اِلَّا اللهُ ص وَلَمْ يُصِرُّوْا عَلٰى مَا فَعَلُوْا وَهُمْ يَعْلَمُوْنَ ۞ اُولٰئِكَ جَزَآؤُهُمْ مَّغْفِرَةٌ مِّنْ رَّبِّهِمْ وَجَنّٰتٌ تَجْرِىْ مِنْ تَحْتِهَا الْاَنْهٰرُ خٰلِدِيْنَ فِيْهَا ۗ وَنِعْمَ اَجْرُ الْعٰمِلِيْنَ ۞

"Hasten towards forgiveness from your Rabb and towards a paradise the width of which spans the heavens and the earth. It has been prepared for the God-fearing: the ones who spend [for Allāh's sake] in prosperity and in adversity, and those who control anger and forgive people. And Allāh loves those who are good in their deeds: those who, when they happen to commit a shameful act or wrong themselves, remember Allāh, then, seek forgiveness

---

[43] Pg. 1825.

for their sins – and who is there to forgive sins except Allāh? And they do not persist in what [wrong] they had done, while they know [the consequences]. Their reward is forgiveness from their Rabb and gardens beneath which rivers flow [paradise] where they shall live forever. And excellent is the reward of those who work [who do righteous deeds according to Allāh's orders].' [44]

Here are some Ahādīth relating to *Istighfaar*:

'O people! Repent to Allāh, for I repent to Him 100 times daily.' [45]

And in one Hadīth Qudsī, Allāh ﷻ says:

'My Servants! You surely sin by night and by day. I forgive all sins, so seek forgiveness from me, I will forgive.'

And:

'Whosoever sticks to Istighfaar, Allāh will grant him relief in all worries and provide a solution for him in every hardship, and will sustain him from where he did not perceive.' [46]

And:

كُلُّ بَنِيْ آدَمَ خَطَّاءٌ وَّخَيْرُ الْخَطَّائِيْنَ التَّوَّابُوْنَ ـ

'The children of Ādam are wrongdoers, but the best of the wrongdoers are the ones who repent.' [47]

---

[44] Qur'ān 3:133-136.
[45] Muslim.
[46] Ahmed, Abū Dāwūd, Ibn Mājah.
[47] Tirmidhī.

And:

$$طُوبٰى لِمَن وَّجَدَ فِيْ صَحِيْفَتِهِ اسْتِغْفَارًا كَثِيْرًا ـ$$

'Glad tidings for him who finds in his book of deeds abundant Istighfaar.' [48]

Bakr Ibn Abdillah says: 'Those who sin the most are the least in seeking forgiveness, whereas those who most often seek forgiveness are the least in committing sins.' [49] A person should constantly seek forgiveness from Allāh ﷻ.

The Prophet ﷺ would say 'Ghufrānak' [I beg your forgiveness] as soon as he would step out of the toilet. [Maybe it was because he was unable to invoke Allāh while relieving himself or because he felt he was unable to do proper shukr for being able to release the harmful stuff from the body].

Abū Bakr Siddīq ؓ requested for a duā by which he could supplicate during salāh. The Prophet ﷺ taught him:

$$اَللّٰهُمَّ اِنِّىْ ظَلَمْتُ نَفْسِىْ ظُلْمًا كَثِيْرًا وَّلَا يَغْفِرُ الذُّنُوْبَ اِلَّا اَنْتَ$$
$$فَاغْفِرْلِىْ مَغْفِرَةً مِّنْ عِنْدِكَ وَارْحَمْنِىْ اِنَّكَ اَنْتَ الْغَفُوْرُ الرَّحِيْمُ ـ$$

O Allāh! Verily I have wronged myself with much wrong, and none can forgive sins except You; so grant me forgiveness from Yourself, and have mercy on me, verily You are oft forgiving, Most Merciful. [50]

The point to note here is that upon completion of the best form of worship, i.e. salāh, we are taught to ask for forgiveness. This is because our worship is not worthy of being put forward in the court of Almighty Allāh ﷻ, however, our salāh which is lacking in proper concentration, is delivered in His courtyard. He accepts and He rewards us too.

---

[48] Ibn Mājah.

[49] Khāzin, pg. 312/4.

[50] Bukhārī.

One could recall here the story of one Bedouin. Once a famine struck a region of Iraq during the time of the *Khalīfāh* Hārūn Rashīd. A Bedouin thought that the *Khalīfāh* must be dying of thirst, so he filled a vessel with some water and brought it to the king. The king opened it, only to see that it was stinking due to the bad smell of the jar. However, he ordered a servant to empty the vessel, fill it with coins and return it to the Bedouin. Thereafter make him pass the river *Dajlah* [Tigris]. When the Bedouin passed by the flowing river, he realised the stupidity of his actions and the generosity of the king, that in spite of having so much clean water, and even though his water had a foul smell, the Khalīfāh not only accepted the water, he also rewarded for it.

It is the generosity of Almighty Allāh ﷻ that He accepts our deeds even though they are worthless. This is why we are taught to seek forgiveness at the end of *salāh*. Even after finishing *salāh*, the Prophet ﷺ would always say '*Astaghfirullāh*' three times. A Hadīth reports:

"When Rasūlullāh ﷺ would complete his salāh, he would seek forgiveness from Allāh three times." [51]

[i.e. say استغفر الله استغفر الله استغفر الله]

May Allāh ﷻ give us the tawfeeq to seek forgiveness from Allāh ﷻ at all times. Āmīn

VERSE 13

﴿مَا لَكُمْ لَا تَرْجُونَ لله وَقَارًا ١٣﴾

What is the matter with you, that ye are not conscious of Allāh's majesty?

The word تَرْجُونَ in this verse holds one of two meanings:

---

[51] Muslim.

1. 'Fear': Thus it could be translated as 'Why do you not fear the majestic power of Almighty Allāh ﷻ?' He has the power to punish you and none can save you from this punishment if He directs it towards you – i.e. what excuse do you have for not fearing Allāh ﷻ?

2. 'Hope': Thus it could mean 'Why do you not hope for the reward promised by Allāh, by showing respect for his commands?'

Ibn Kaysān says: 'What is the matter with you that you do not hope through Allāh's worship and obedience that He will reward you for the respect you show to Him?'

Ibn Abbās, Saeed Ibn Jubayr, Abul-Āliya and some other *Mufassireen* have taken both meanings at the same time – they interpret it thus: 'Why do you not hope for His reward and fear His wrath?'

Imām Hassan Basrī says: 'Why do you not realise His due rights and pay homage for His bounties?'

Qurtubī narrates from some who say: 'Why do you not unify His being?' Because when one shows respect to Allāh ﷻ, then it means that he believes that Allāh ﷻ is the only Supreme Being – maybe this is why Sayyidunā Nūh ﷺ mentions some signs of His oneness in the following verses.

VERSE 14

وَقَدْ خَلَقَكُمْ أَطْوَارًا ﴿١٤﴾

"Even though (you know) He created you in stages."

Qurtubī ﷺ says: 'This means that Allāh has kept a sign of his oneness within yourselves.'

Allāh ﷻ says in Sūrah Hā Meem Sajdāh:

$$\text{سَنُرِيهِمْ اٰيٰتِنَا فِى الْاٰفَاقِ وَفِىْ اَنْفُسِهِمْ} ۞$$

"Soon We shall show them our signs in the world,
as well as within themselves." [52]

And in Sūrah Zāriyāt:

$$\text{وَفِى الْاَرْضِ اٰيٰتٌ لِّلْمُوْقِنِيْنَ} ۞$$

$$\text{وَفِىْ اَنْفُسِكُمْ ۚ اَفَلَا تُبْصِرُوْنَ} ۞$$

"And in the Earth there are signs for those who have
sure faith, and within yourselves. Do you not see?' [53]

'Stages' here is interpreted in different ways:

1. The development of the foetus in the womb, from a
drop of semen, to a clot of blood, to a chewed-like
substance [piece of meat], to putting on bones and
skin until He made you a complete human being.

Allāh ﷻ says in Sūrah Al-Mu'minūn:

$$\text{وَلَقَدْ خَلَقْنَا الْاِنْسَانَ مِنْ سُلٰلَةٍ مِّنْ طِيْنٍ} ۞ \text{ثُمَّ جَعَلْنٰهُ نُطْفَةً فِىْ قَرَارٍ مَّكِيْنٍ}$$

$$۞ \text{ثُمَّ خَلَقْنَا النُّطْفَةَ عَلَقَةً فَخَلَقْنَا الْعَلَقَةَ مُضْغَةً فَخَلَقْنَا الْمُضْغَةَ عِظٰمًا}$$

$$\text{فَكَسَوْنَا الْعِظٰمَ لَحْمًا ۚ ثُمَّ اَنْشَأْنٰهُ خَلْقًا اٰخَرَ ۚ}$$

$$\text{فَتَبٰرَكَ اللهُ اَحْسَنُ الْخٰلِقِيْنَ} ۞$$

---

[52] Qur'ān 41:53.
[53] Qur'ān 51:20-21.

"We created man from a quintessence [of clay]. Then we placed him [as a drop of] sperm in a place of rest, firmly fixed. Then we made the sperm into a clot of congealed blood; then of that clot, we made a foetus: lump; then out of the lump we made bones and clothed the bones with flesh; then we developed out of it [a completely different] creature. So, blessed be Allāh, the best of makers." [54]

2. The development of a human being through his life stages means from babies to children, to young men, to old men, i.e. weak, and then strong and energetic, and then weak again.

3. أَطْوَارُ here could mean of different types, i.e. healthy and sick, blind and seeing, rich and poor.

4. It could mean with different characters, i.e. good and bad and of a different nature. [55]

Here the second and third interpretations seem more appropriate because Sayyidunā Nūh ﷺ is trying to divert their attention towards something evident within themselves. For this, it would be wise to tell them something which they can all understand. The stages of an embryo are not known to individuals and therefore they cannot take any lessons from that. However, the differences of ages, energy, health and wealth point towards their one Creator, because if there was no Creator and the world came about through its own accord then all the humans would be the same, just like a machine when it is set to make a certain product, it will keep on creating the same product that it has been programmed to create, so the differences of human beings, in their creation, actions, manners, etc., point towards their Creator, and this can be understood by any layman.

---

[54] Qur'ān 23:12-14.
[55] Qurtubī, pg. 303-19.

VERSE 15

اَلَمْ تَرَوْا كَيْفَ خَلَقَ اللهُ سَبْعَ سَمٰوٰتٍ طِبَاقًا ﴿١٥﴾

"Have you not seen how Allāh has created the seven heavens
above one another?"

Another proof of God's existence is put before them, i.e. do you not
realise that the one who has the power to do this is the one who
deserves to be worshipped?

Allāmā Uthmānī ﷺ says: 'The heavens are formed like concrete
circles one upon the other.'

Allāmā Qurtubī ﷺ writes: 'Do you not see?' means, 'Do you not
know?'

There are seven skies over us, one above the other. The Hadīth of
me'rāj explains this. Rasūlullāh ﷺ went through them one after the
other. Jibra'īl ﷺ was with him. He also met many prophets there.

VERSE 16

وَجَعَلَ الْقَمَرَ فِيهِنَّ نُوْرًا وَّجَعَلَ الشَّمْسَ سِرَاجًا ﴿١٦﴾

"And He has placed the moon therein for light,
And has made the sun as a burning lamp."

Allāmā Uthmānī ﷺ writes, 'The light of the sun is fast and hot. Its
appearance in the morning removes the darkness of night. This is
perhaps why it is likened to a burning lamp. And the light of the moon
is but the expansion of the light of the same burning lamp that
becomes cool and thin due to the medium of the lunar body [Allāh
knows best].'

When Nūh ﷺ was preaching to the nation, there were no scientific
resources for research. Since the sun and the moon, and the signs of

Allāh ﷻ within them are apparent and clear, Nūh ﷺ drew their attention towards these amazing creations of Allāh ﷻ so that they may ponder over them and turn towards their Creator.

In today's advanced era, we learn through science that the sun and moon both have a huge effect on the lives of the inhabitants of the Earth. The sun provides the Earth with light. Its light is the source of growth for plants and vegetation, which in turn become the food of animals and man. The rising of the sun brings daylight for us and its setting brings the darkness of night. Its journey from east to west helps in determining time. The sun's rotation provides all parts of the world with light and darkness, giving people and animals protection from the sun's intense heat in the hotter parts of the world. Its rotating provides shade in one place at one time and later on in the day at the same place it provides light.

The sun's heat travels to us from millions of miles away. The heat's intensity varies through different parts of the world and during different seasons.

The sun is also a source of power and energy for the Earth. Solar panels are used to take in solar rays from the sun and this energy is used in some vehicles and for various other purposes.

The moon is a means of telling the date [lunar calendar]. The moon has its own gravity which pulls the oceans and the seas, causing the tide to rise and fall. It also causes the waves which are used to produce hydro-electricity.

VERSES 17–18

﴿١٧﴾ وَاللّٰهُ أَنْبَتَكُم مِّنَ الْأَرْضِ نَبَاتًا

﴿١٨﴾ ثُمَّ يُعِيْدُكُمْ فِيْهَا وَيُخْرِجُكُمْ اِخْرَاجًا

"And Allāh has produced you from the earth, growing [gradually]. And in the End, He will return you into the earth and raise you forth [again at resurrection]."

Allāmā Uthmānī ﷺ writes, 'He created you from the earth cohesively with implantation. First our father, Ādam, was created of mud, then the sperm-drop, which is the matter of human creation, is the substance of the earth. In structure, man is an embodiment of coherent organs. Similarly, his talents and powers are coherent. His strength depends upon his cohesive formation and structure.'

After death, men are mixed with the earth, then after Qiyāmah, they shall be brought forth from it.

Almighty Allāh ﷻ has implanted vitamins and minerals into the soil, which provide nutrition for the human body. Herbalists say that today's crops have become corrupted by the chemicals and fertilisers used in planting. Therefore, grains and vegetables do not provide enough vitamins for the human body, thus we need to take vitamins in other forms to correct the imbalance in our diet.

VERSES 19 – 20

وَاللهُ جَعَلَ لَكُمُ الْأَرْضَ بِسَاطًا ﴿١٩﴾

لِّتَسْلُكُوْا مِنْهَا سُبُلًا فِجَاجًا ﴿٢٠﴾

And Allāh has laid out the earth as a carpet for you. So you may travel around on highways which lead through mountain passes.

After discussing the heavens, Sayyidunā Nūh ﷺ turned their attention to the earth when he said, 'And Allāh has made the earth a bedding for you so that you can travel in its wide roads.' Despite its spherical structure, Allāh ﷻ has made the earth as flat as a bed for man so that he can travel easily throughout the earth to fulfil his various needs. Allāh ﷻ has placed the earth at man's service so that he may derive benefit from its resources. Allāh ﷻ says in Sūrah Mulk:

هُوَ الَّذِىْ جَعَلَ لَكُمُ الْأَرْضَ ذَلُوْلًا فَامْشُوْا فِىْ مَنَاكِبِهَا وَكُلُوْا مِنْ رِّزْقِهٖ ۞

"It is He who subjugated the earth for you so you can walk on its road and eat from His sustenance." [56]

The above verse does not denote that the earth is flat and not spherical in shape. The same applies to other verses as well, such as verse 6 of Sūrah Naba [57] and verse 20 of Sūrah Ghāshiya [58]. These verses describe the earth from a man's point of view as he stands on the earth, which appears flat to him. These verses emphasise that although the earth is spherical in shape, Allāh ﷻ has not allowed this to affect man's existence on the surface. It should be noted that believing that the earth has a spherical shape or not believing this has no bearing on the *sharī'ah*. No verse of the Qur'ān refutes this belief. [59]

VERSES 21–22

قَالَ نُوْحٌ رَّبِّ اِنَّهُمْ عَصَوْنِىْ وَاتَّبَعُوْا مَنْ لَّمْ يَزِدْهُ مَالُهٗ

وَوَلَدُهٗ اِلَّا خَسَارًا ﴿٢١﴾ وَمَكَرُوْا مَكْرًا كُبَّارًا ﴿٢٢﴾

Nūh ﷺ said, "My Rabb, they have defied me and followed after someone whose wealth and children will only increase [them in loss]. And they devised a tremendous plot."

Sayyidunā Nūh's ﷺ wonderful speech concludes on verse 20. However, people do not like preachers. They did not pay the slightest

---

[56] Qur'ān 67:15.
[57] Qur'ān 78.
[58] Qur'ān 88.
[59] Anwarul Bayān, Vol.10, Pg. 95.

of attention to the advices given by Nūh ﷺ. Instead, they made fun of him and abused him. When many years passed in this state, and Nūh ﷺ lost all hope of their rectification, he pleaded to his Rabb Almighty with the following words:

He said: 'O Allāh! My people disobeyed me when I told them to believe in You and to seek forgiveness from You. They preferred the path of the wealthy and haughty people, whose wealth only increases their pride and big-headedness, and thus results in great loss. They have made great plots in undermining my position, degrading me, and driving people away from me.'

Allāmā Uthmānī ﷺ writes: 'They followed their wealthy Lords and *Amīrs*, in whose wealth there is no blessing or betterment, nay, but their wealth is a misfortune for them. Due to their wealth and possessions they deprived themselves of practicing the true religion and also deprived others due to their haughtiness and arrogance. They did not stop here. They advised all their men and women not to pay any heed to my sermons and lectures and that they should hurt me and annoy me in various ways.' [60]

This was the condition of the disbelievers for what some might call the 'Stone Age.' We can see that the disbelievers of this age are also the same. They devise tremendous plots to drive people away from the path of Allāh. The media is the greatest tool. People have become so vulnerable that they believe anything and everything they are told. No matter how clear the fabrication is, people follow their lead. However, not all is lost. The people of the European countries we live in are much wiser in comparison to others. They have better educational systems and access to education for the masses. They understand things better. Therefore, it is our duty, as Muslims, to propagate the truth in order to reach out to people who are searching for the truth. May Allāh ﷻ give us the *Tawfeeq* and ability to do so. Āmīn!

---

[60] Tafsīr Uthmānī, Vol.3, Pg.2457.

VERSE 23

وَقَالُوا لَا تَذَرُنَّ اٰلِهَتَكُمْ وَلَا تَذَرُنَّ وَدًّا وَلَا

سُوَاعًا لَا وَلَا يَغُوْثَ وَيَعُوْقَ وَنَسْرًا ﴿٢٣﴾

And they said: "Never forsake your gods, and do not leave
Wadd nor Suwa, nor Yaguth, Ya'ouk, and Nasr."

They advised their folk to be steadfast in supporting their gods and
not to be deceived by Nūh ﷺ. The *Mufassireen* say that Prophet Nūh
ﷺ had a very long life and called upon his people for a period of 950
years, as mentioned in the Qur'ān. However, his people did not have
the same lifespan. At least three generations expired before
Sayyidunā Nūh ﷺ. So whenever a father was about to die, he would
advise his children and grandchildren not to go anywhere near 'that
old man', nor to leave the traditional religion of their forefathers.

Wadd, Suwa, Yaguth, Ya'ouk and *Nasr* are the names of their idols,
Ibn Abbās ﷺ says these were the names of holy men. When they died,
Shaytān inspired his followers to make their pictures, in order to
remember them. Then he ordered them to make their statues and
place them in their places of assembly. Soon people started to revere
these statues. And when the next generation came, they started to
worship the statues. This is how idol worship started. This is one of
the reasons taking pictures of living things is prohibited in Islam, i.e.
it could lead to the worship of pictures.

Ibn Abbās ﷺ says that these same idols were brought to Arabia as
well. *Wadd* belonged to Banū Kalb in *Dawmatul Jandal*. *Suwā* belonged
to Huzail, *Yagūth* to Muraad, *Ya'ouk* to Hamdhaan, and *Nasr* to the
Himyar. There were also other idols among the Arabs, e.g. *Laat, Uzzā,
Manāt*. The Arabs would keep their names by relating to these idols,
e.g. Abd Wadd, Abd Yagūth, Abd Uzzā, etc.

Khāzin has narrated from Ibn Abbās ﷺ that the flood had buried those idols under the soil. They remained buried until Shaytān brought them out for the *Mushrikeen* of Arabia.

Allāmā Uthmānī ﷺ says: 'The same kind of idols came to India as well. They are famous by the names of Vishnu, Brahma, Shiva, and Hanuman, etc.'

Hadhrat Shah Abdul Aziz ﷺ has given some details in his *Tasfīr Fathul Aziz*. He writes that the *mushrikeen* had deemed the idols to be the *Mazāhir* of *Tajjallīyāte Rabbānīyyah*. [61]

'*Wadd*' was thought to be the *mazhar* [manifestation] of love. The word is derived from '*mawaddat*', which means love. God has created this world and He loves His creation as mentioned in many narrations. The people of Nūh ﷺ made an idol as a manifestation of God's love. The Hindus also have a similar idol by the name of 'Rati' and 'Kamadeva'.

'*Suwaa*' indicates towards standing firm and being strong. God is self-existent and gives existence to the universe. This could be something similar to '*Al-Qayyoom*' in the name of Allāh. The idolaters of Nūh's tribe had made this idol in the form of a woman, maybe because it is she upon whom depends the existence of the household. The Hindus call this god 'Brahma'.

'*Yagūth*' means to help, assist and aid. To assist in one's hour of need is the attribute of God Almighty. The people of Nūh ﷺ had made this god in the shape of a horse, maybe because it was a very fast runner and provides succour at the time of need. The Hindus call this god 'Indra'.

'*Ya'ouk*' means to stop, prevent. Protecting from calamities is the attribute of Almighty God. The people of Nūh ﷺ had made this idol in the form of a lion, maybe because a lion protects its cubs from other beasts in such a manner that no one dares to approach them. Also,

---

[61] Mazhaar: Object in which something manifests itself. Tajallī: Manifestation. Rabbānīyyah: Divine, Godly. Thus Mushrikeen believed that the idols were 'objects of divine manifestation'.

when a lion confronts another beast, it has no choice but to run off. The Hindus call this god 'Shiva'.

'Nasr' means eagle or vulture. This idol was the mazhar of the power of God. A vulture is famous for its powers among the birds, also it flies at a considerable speed. This could be why the people of Nūh ﷺ had made this idol in the form of a vulture. The Hindus call this god 'Hanuman.'

Shah Sahib also writes that the word 'La' [i.e. nor] is repeated with 'Wadd' and 'Suwaa' whereas 'Yagūth', 'Ya'ouk' and 'Nasr' are mentioned under one 'La'. The reason for this is that the latter three were thought to be gods of the same quality, which is taking care of the universe, whereas 'Wadd' is related to the creation of the universe and 'Suwaa' to the existence of it.

The Mushrikeen committed these polytheistic acts due to delusive imagination [wahm]. Some ignorant people who call themselves Muslims would make a statue of Hadhrat Alī ibn Abī Tālib ﷺ in the form of a lion, simply because he was nicknamed 'Asadullāh' [the Lion of God].

VERSE 24

وَقَدْ اَضَلُّوْا كَثِيْرًا ج وَلَا تَزِدِ الظّٰلِمِيْنَ اِلَّا ضَلٰلًا ﴿٢٤﴾

"Surely they have thus far misled many. So do not let the unjust increase in anything but misguidance."

Nūh ﷺ says, 'The elders of the tribe have already led many of the ignorant ones astray. This is in keeping with what he said prior to this, 'they have devised a plot.'

Qurtubī says, 'By "they" the indication could be towards the idols, i.e. the idols have mislead.' This is the same as Ibrāhīm ﷺ had said:

رَبِّ اِنَّهُنَّ اَضْلَلْنَ كَثِيْرًا مِّنَ النَّاسِ ۞

'O My Rabb, the idols have mislead many people.' [62]

Abdullāh Yūsuf Alī writes, 'Such pagan superstitions and cults do not add to human knowledge or human well-being. They only increase error and wrongdoing. For example, how much lewdness resulted from the Greek and Roman Saturnalia! And how much lewdness results from ribald Holi songs! This is the natural result, and Nūh in his bitterness of spirit prays that Allāh's Grace may be cut off from the men who hung them to their hearts. They mislead others: Let them miss their own mark.' [63]

Ibn Kathīr ﷺ writes: 'They mislead many through the idols that they invented, to the point where this idol worship remains in consistence up to the present day, throughout the Arabs as well as the *Ajam* [non-Arabs].' Ibrāhim *Khalīlullāh* ﷺ said in his duā: 'My Rabb they have mislead many people.' [64]

Even in the modern world, one sees millions of people being misled through idol-worship. The Bollywood film industry is booming and may have already overtaken Hollywood in terms of viewers and profits. No Indian film is free from idol-worship. It is not uncommon to see actors with Islamic names bowing in front of idols. Even those in the Arab world who do not understand a word of the Hindi language are fascinated by such films, due to the music, lyrics, and dancing that comprise these films. The amount of idol-worship contained in these films is mind-boggling. The viewer begins to make light of this ritual and sometimes even develops an inclination towards it.

One must remember that Allāh ﷻ has declared very clearly in the Qur'ān in numerous verses that He forgives all types of sins except for *shirk*. He has proclaimed in the clearest possible manner that He will never forgive *shirk*, and that a *mushrik* will have to dwell in the hellfire forever and ever. Therefore, one must always be fearful of his fate.

---

[62] Qur'ān 14:36.

[63] Pg. 1287.

[64] Vol.3, Pg. 554.

One must avoid these things lest they annihilate his *Īmān*. One must try to be punctual of his five daily *salāh*, recite some Qur'ān regularly, and also perform some *dhikr* without fail in order to preserve their *Īmān*. One should also give lots of *sadaqah*, because *sadaqah* defuses the wrath of Allāh ﷻ. May Allāh ﷻ give us the *tawfeeq* and keep us steadfast upon *Īmān* and good actions.

Here, Prophet Nūh ﷺ first mentions that the idols have mislead many people and then he curses the oppressors by the words, 'And do not increase the unjust ones [the tyrants], except in straying from the mark.'

The *Mufassireen* have put forward the question as to why a Prophet would curse his people.

The answer is that Nūh ﷺ was informed by Allāh ﷻ that:

$$\text{اَنَّهُ لَنْ يُّؤْمِنَ مِنْ قَوْمِكَ اِلَّا مَنْ قَدْ اٰمَنَ}$$

'None of your folk will believe except for those who have already believed.' [65]

He had maintained his patience for 950 years. Today one cannot even keep patience for a few minutes, let alone years.

Mūsā ﷺ kept his patience with Fir'awn. However, when he realised that Fir'awn would never turn towards the truth, and would only mislead others by preventing them from accepting the truth, he supplicated:

$$\text{رَبَّنَا اطْمِسْ عَلٰى اَمْوَالِهِمْ وَاشْدُدْ عَلٰى قُلُوْبِهِمْ}$$
$$\text{فَلَا يُؤْمِنُوْا حَتّٰى يَرَوُا الْعَذَابَ الْاَلِيْمَ}$$

'Our Rabb! Wipe out their wealth and harden their hearts

---

[65] Qur'ān 11:36.

so they might not believe until they see the painful torment.' [66]

Nūh's ﷺ patience is also remarkable. It was only when he was told that no good was to come out from the people or from their offspring that he raised his hands and made the above supplication.

VERSE 25

مِّمَّا خَطِيْئَاتِهِمْ اُغْرِقُوْا فَاُدْخِلُوْا نَارًا لَا

فَلَمْ يَجِدُوْا لَهُمْ مِّنْ دُوْنِ الله اَنْصَارًا ﴿٢٥﴾

"Because of their sins, they were drowned [in the flood] and were thrust into the fire, and they found that besides Allāh there was none that could help them."

"Because of their sins..." Their major sins were *kufr* and *shirk*. *Kufr* means denial of the Creator, and *shirk* means associating partners with Him. Besides this, they had also accumulated many other major sins.

Nasafī ﷺ writes, 'In mentioning their sinning before their drowning, and being pushed in the fire, there is an indication, that the only reason for their punishment was their grave sins. In this, there is a grave warning for those who commit major sins, e.g. adultery, stealing, drinking, gambling, murdering, etc.'

"They were drowned and made to enter the fire." The detail of their drowning has been mentioned in Sūrah Hūd from verse 36 to verse 49. Allāh ﷻ says:

---

[66] Qur'ān 10:88.

'It was revealed to Nūh ☙ that: None of your folk will ever believe except for those who have already believed. Do not despair about what they have been doing. Build the Ark under our eyes and our inspiration. Do not talk to me about those who have done wrong; they will be drowned.

As he was building the Ark, each time any gentleman from his own people passed by him, they would sneer at him. He said, 'If you ridicule us, then we will ridicule you just the way you are sneering. You will come to know who will be given torment which will shame him, and have lasting torment settle down upon him.'

So when Our command came and the bowels [of the earth] welled up, we said 'Load her [Ark] with two apiece from every species, and your own family - except for anyone against whom the sentence has already been pronounced – also [load] those who have believed.' Yet only a few believed along with him.

He said, 'Board her: In the name of God, her sailing and her mooring; my Rabb is Forgiving, Merciful!'

She sailed on with them through waves that were like mountains. Nūh ☙ called out to his son who stood aloof by himself, 'My dear son! Come on board with us, and do not stay with the disbelievers,' He said, 'I will take refuge on a mountain which will protect me from the water. He said, 'Nothing can protect you from Allāh's command except for someone on whom He shows mercy. A wave swept in between them so he was one of those who were drowned.

[Then after some time] It was said, 'Earth! Swallow your water!' and 'Sky clear up!', so the water receded, the command was accomplished and she settled down on Mount Judi, it was said, away with the wrongdoing folk!'

Nūh ﷺ called upon his Rabb and said, 'My Rabb! My son belonged to my own family, while your promise is true, and you are the wisest Judge!' He replied, 'Nūh ﷺ, He was not of your family: indeed his deeds were not righteous, so do not ask Me about which you have no knowledge; I advise you lest you may be among the ignorant.' He said, 'My Rabb I take refuge with You from asking that of which I have no knowledge. If You do not forgive me and show me mercy, I will be among the losers.' It was said, 'Nūh ﷺ! Disembark with peace from Us; and blessings upon you and upon nations [descending] from those with you. But other nations [of them], We will grant enjoyment; then painful torment from Us will afflict them.' This is some of the news of the unseen, which We reveal to you [O Muhammad!]. Neither you nor your people knew it before this, so be patient. The outcome belongs to those who do their duty.'

As to whether this flood was global or regional, there are two opinions: Shaykh Hifzur-Rahmān Suyuharwī ﷺ writes in *Qasasul Qur'ān*:

> 1. 'A group of Islamic Scholars, the learned people of Jews and Christians, some experts of astronomy, and geology are of the opinion that this flood was not for the whole of the Earth. Rather it came upon that particular area where Nūh ﷺ was sent as a Prophet. This area is approximately 140,000 square kilometres. Their argument is that if it came upon the whole of the earth, then its effects should be found all over the world. Also during that time, mankind was limited to that area only. The children of Ādam had not spread to all parts of the world. Therefore, the only people who deserved that punishment were the ones staying in that area.'

2. Other Ulamā and experts of geography and professors of nature say that the flood was global. They say that other than the areas where Nūh ﷺ was sent, we have found in many mountains, bones and parts of animals which live in water. It would have been impossible for them to come out of the water and climb up the mountains. Therefore, the only explanation could be that a huge flood came and the water took them to those heights and after the water receded, they died there. Ibn Khaldun has mentioned in his 'Tareekh' that it was global. *Tasfīr Mawāhibur-Rahmān* also states the same.

Allāmā Shabbīr Ahmed Uthmānī ﷺ writes: 'Dairatul-Maarif has narrated from many European researchers that this flood was global. Most of them also believe that the human beings are now descendants of Nūh's ﷺ three sons; Haam, Saam and Yafith.'

The Qur'ān also states:

$$وَجَعَلْنَا ذُرِّيَّتَهُ هُمُ الْبَاقِيْنَ ۞$$

'We have made his descendants the only ones to remain.' [67]

Shah Abdul Aziz Muhaddith Dehlawī ﷺ writes: 'There is none among the *Salaf* or the *Khalaf* who say that the flood was regional. The opinion of the Jews is not worthy of mention. Even though Nūh's ﷺ message was not universal, his tribe were the only inhabitants of the earth at that time. The earth was not inhabited as it is today. So when the flood came, it wiped out the whole creation off the face of the Earth. The whole world was drowned and only those remained who boarded the ship with Sayyidunā Nūh ﷺ. If someone were to object as to how can such a huge population come into existence from the few people

---

[67] Qur'ān 37:77.

boarding the ship, they should remember that we are all children of Ādam and Hawā [Peace be upon them].' [68]

"They were pushed into the fire..." Imām Qurtubī narrates from Ustādh Abul Qāsim Al Qushayrī ☙ that this depicts the punishment of the grave.

Dhahhāk says: 'They were punished by the fire in this world along with the drowning in this world, all at the same time. On one side they were drowning and on the other side they were burning.'

Abdullāh Yūsuf Alī writes: 'The punishment of the sin seizes the soul from every side in every form. Water [drowning] indicates death by suffocation, through the nose, ears, eyes, mouth and lungs. Fire has the opposite effect: it burns the skin, the limbs, the flesh, the brain, the bones, and every part of the body. So the destruction wrought by sin is complete from all points of view.'

Some who deny 'azābul qabr' [the chastisement in the grave] say, this means they made themselves worthy of azāb or the places in the fire of hell were open in front of them:

$$ اَلنَّارُ يُعْرَضُوْنَ عَلَيْهَا غُدُوًّا وَّعَشِيًّا ۞ $$

'In front of the fire, they will be brought morning and evening.' [69]

Azābul qabr is mentioned in numerous verses of the Qur'ān as well as in a number of Ahādīth.

Here are a few quotes regarding *azābul qabr* [punishment in the grave]:

1. Ā'ishah ☙ told of a Jewess who visited her and mentioned the punishment in the grave adding, 'May God protect you from the punishment of the grave!'

---

[68] Fatāwā Azīzīya, Pg.47, Gulalaste Tasfīr, Vol.3, Pg.370.
[69] Qur'ān 40:46.

Ā'ishah ﷺ asked God's messenger ﷺ about the subject and he said, 'Yes, the punishment in the grave is real.' Ā'ishah ﷺ said, 'After that I never saw God's messenger observing a prayer without seeking God's protection from the punishment in the grave.' [70]

2. Zaid ibn Thābit said: While we were accompanying God's Messenger ﷺ who was riding a she-mule in a garden belonging to Banu-Najjār, the animal began to jump up and almost unseated him. It happened that there were five or six graves there, so he asked if anyone knew who were buried in them. A man replied that he did, and on being asked when they died, he said it was in the period when the people were polytheists. The Prophet ﷺ then said, 'These people are being afflicted in their graves, and were it not that you would cease to bury, I would ask God to let you hear the punishment in the grave which I am hearing.' Then he turned facing us and said, 'Seek refuge in God from the punishment of the fire.' They said, 'We seek refuge in God from the punishment of the fire.' He said, 'Seek refuge in God from the punishment of the grave.' They said, 'We seek refuge in God from the punishment of the grave.' He said, 'Seek refuge in God from trials, both open and secret.' They said, 'We seek refuge in God from trials, both open and secret.' He said, 'Seek refuge in God from the trial of ad-Dajjāl.' They said, 'We seek refuge in God from the trials of ad-Dajjāl.' [71]

---

[70] Bukhārī, Muslim.
[71] Muslim.

3. Abū Hurairah ﷺ reported God's Messenger ﷺ as saying, 'When the deceased is buried, two black and blue angels, one is called al-Munkar and the other an-Nakīr, come to him and ask him what opinion he held about this man. If he is a believer he replies, 'He is the servant and messenger of God. I testify that there is no God but Allāh and Muhammad is His servant and apostle.' They say that they knew he would say so. A space of 4,900 square cubits is then made for him in his grave, it is illuminated for him and he is told to sleep. He will then express a desire to return to his family to tell them, but he will be told to sleep like one newly married who is awakened only by the member of his family who is dearest to him until God resurrects him from his resting place. But if he is a hypocrite, he will say, 'I heard men expressing a belief and I held the same, but I really do not know.' They will tell him they knew he would say so; then the earth will be told to press in upon him and it will do so. His ribs will be compressing together and he will remain there suffering punishment till God resurrects him from that resting place of his.' [72]

4. When Uthmān ﷺ stood over a grave, he would weep so sorely that the tears moistened his beard. Someone said to him, 'You talk about Paradise and Hell, without weeping, yet you are weeping over this?' He replied that God's Messenger ﷺ said, 'The grave is the first stage of the next world; if one escapes from it, what follows will be made easy for him. However, if he is caught up here then what follows will be more severe

---

[72] Tirmidhī.

than it.' He further quoted God's messenger ﷺ as saying, 'I have never seen a sight as horrible as the grave.' [73]

5. He also said that when the Prophet ﷺ finished the burial of the dead, he stood over it and said, 'Ask forgiveness for your brother, then ask that he may be kept steadfast, for he is now being questioned.' [74]

6. Abu Hurairah ؓ reported God's Messenger ﷺ as saying, 'Ninety-nine serpents will be given power over an infidel in his grave, and will bite and sting him till the last hour comes. If one of those serpents were to breathe over the earth, it would bring forth no green thing.' [75]

"There was none that could help them..." Wadd, Suwaa, Yagūth, Ya'ouk, and Nasr, their idols could not save them from the chastisement of Allāh ﷻ.

VERSE 26

وَقَالَ نُوحٌ رَّبِّ لَا تَذَرْ عَلَى الْأَرْضِ مِنَ الْكَٰفِرِيْنَ دَيَّارًا ﴿٢٦﴾

Nūh ؑ said, "O My Rabb! Do not leave upon the earth one inhabited house of the Disbelievers."

---

[73] Sunan Tirmidhī and Sunan Ibn Mājah transmitted it, Sunan Tirmidhī said this is a *gharīb* tradition.

[74] Abū Dāwūd.

[75] Dārimī transmitted it, and Tirmidhī transmitted something similar, but he said seventy instead of ninety-nine.

This means that O my Rabb, since you have promised to accept my duā regarding these people, then I plead to you not to let any single *kāfir* soul wander around the earth. Nūh ﷺ has been informed that none will believe except those who had already believed.

Allāh ﷺ used the word '*dayyār*' which is derived from '*daarā*' which means to 'turn around' or 'to roam around', i.e. any disbeliever roaming around the earth. This is because Nūh ﷺ knew that Shaytān and his progeny had been given respite until the Day of Judgement, therefore he could not include them in his *duā*, and since Shaytān and his progeny live in the oceans and highlands, and fly around in the air rather than walk on the earth, he used the word '*dayyār*'.

VERSE 27

اِنَّكَ اِنْ تَذَرْهُمْ يُضِلُّوْا عِبَادَكَ وَلَا يَلِدُوْا اِلَّا فَاجِرًا كَفَّارًا ﴿٢٧﴾

"Definitely if Thou leave them, they will lead Thy servants astray, and they will breed none but the obstinate, disbelievers."

Allāmā Uthmānī ﷺ writes: 'Sayyidunā Nūh ﷺ prayed, O My Rabb! If any of them exists, my experience is that from his single sperm-drop only the obstinate, impudent, unthankful, and disbelievers in truth shall be created, and as far as any one of them survives, he will lead others astray, not to speak of his own guidance.'

Ibn Kathīr says: 'Nūh ﷺ had stayed with them for nearly a thousand years and therefore he had gained a considerable amount of experience regarding their attitude.'

He also writes, 'Allāh accepted Nūh's ﷺ duā. He destroyed each and every disbeliever who had inhabited the earth, even Nūh's own flesh and blood, his son, who had refused to accept his father's way of life. He said to his father, 'I will seek refuge upon a mountain which will protect me from drowning.'

Ibn Abbās 🙵 narrates that the Prophet ﷺ said, If Allāh were to have mercy on anyone from the people of Nūh, He would have shown mercy to that woman who upon seeing water, held her son in her hands, then climbed the mountain. When water reached her, she lifted him upon her shoulders. When the water approached her shoulders, she lifted him upon her head. When the water reached her head, she raised him with her hands. So if Allāh were to have mercy on anyone of them. He would have had mercy on this woman.'

No one was saved from this punishment except for the people of the ship who had believed in Nūh 🙵 and who had been commanded to board the ship by none other than Allāh 🙵 himself.

VERSE 28

رَّبِّ اغْفِرْ لِيْ وَلِوَالِدَيَّ وَلِمَنْ دَخَلَ بَيْتِيَ مُؤْمِنًا

وَّلِلْمُؤْمِنِيْنَ وَالْمُؤْمِنٰتِ ط وَلَا تَزِدِ الظّٰلِمِيْنَ اِلَّا تَبَارًا ﴿٢٨﴾

"O My Rabb! Forgive me and my parents and whosoever enters my house
as a believer and all believing men and all believing women, and to the
wrong-doers grant Thou no increase but in ruin."

"Forgive me..." Prophets are *mā'sūm* [sinless]; they never ever disobey a single command of Allāh 🙵. In spite of this they stand motionless in front of Allāh 🙵. They show utmost respect and humility by supplicating to Him in all circumstances and by seeking His forgiveness for the slightest mistake that might have occurred unintentionally, without realising. It is said, 'The closer you are the more fearful you will be.' Since the Prophets are the closest to Allāh 🙵, they fear the most. This is why they seek forgiveness abundantly.

"...And my parents..." 'Khāzin narrates that his father's name was 'Lamak ibn Matushlak' and his mother's name was 'Shamkaa bint

Anush', and they were both believers. Some have said that between Ādam and Nūh ﷺ there are ten fathers and none of them was a disbeliever.

"And whoever enters my house..." Dhahhāk says, 'My home means the masjid.' Some say it means 'my ship'. Ibn Kathīr's opinion is that it could be a general term referring to his house. Imām Ahmad narrates a Hadīth, 'Do not befriend anyone but a believer and do not let anyone eat your food except for the god-fearing.'

"...And all the believers..." Male and female, this includes every believer who is to come until the Last day, those who are alive as well as those who have died. Ibn Kathīr says it is *Mustahab* [desirable] to say this *Duā*, following the footsteps of Nūh ﷺ.

Allāmā Uthmānī ﷺ prays, 'O Allāh! By the blessings of Nūh's ﷺ prayer, forgive this sinful one as well and forgive all Thy servants by Thy mercy, and grant us entry into paradise without any 'Hisāb' [Reckoning]. Verily Thou art All-hearing, All-mighty, and All-accepting.'

امين بحرمة سيد المرسلين صلوات الله

وسلامه عليه وعلى اله واصحابه اجمعين ـ

[The Tasfīr of Sūrah Nūh has ended by His Grace and Kindness]

GLOSSARY

A
Ahlul Hadith: People of the Hadīth
Ahlul Qur'ān: People of the Qur'ān
Al Muttaqūn: God-conscious people
Alayhī Salaam: Peace be upon him
Alhamdulillāh: All praises due to Allāh
Ālim: Islamic Scholar
Amal-e-sālih: Good actions
Āmīn: O Allāh accept our invocation
Amīrs: Leaders
Astaghfirullāh: I seek forgiveness from Allāh
Āyah: Verse
Azābul Qabr: Punishment of the grave

B
Banū Isrā'īl: Israelites

D
Dāees: Callers to Allāh
Dajjāl: False Messiah, Anti-Christ
Da'wah: Invitation, propagation
Dā'wat: Invitation
Deen: Religion
Dhaeef: Weak
Dhikr: Remembrance of God
Duā: Supplication

F

Fatwā: Religious verdict

Fardh: Compulsory

Fiqh: The understanding and application of Islamic ideas, laws, commandments etc. from original sources of shari'ah

Fuqahā: Jurists, one who has external knowledge and experience in the field of Fiqh

Furū': Subsidiary issues

G

Gharīb: Hadīth which is reported by only one narrator at any level of its chain

Ghufraanak: O God we seek your pardon

H

Hadīth: [Plural: Ahādīth] originally means a piece of news, story, or a report relating to a past or present event. In the technical meaning, it stands for the report of the words and deeds, approval or disapproval of Rasūlullāh ﷺ. In other words, the saying, action, or consent of Rasūlullāh ﷺ.

Hajj: Pilgrimage

Hanafi: A person who follows the school of Fiqh related to the great Imām Abū Hanīfa ﷽.

Harām: Unlawful, forbidden and punishable from the view point of religion.

Harbī: Living in Dārul-Harb

Hidayaat: Guidance

Hisāb: Account

I

Ibaadah: To worship

Imām: The person who leads others in salāh or Muslim caliph

Īmān: Faith

Istighfaar: Seeking forgiveness
Istisqaa: Specific prayer for drought

K
Kāfir: Disbeliever, one who rejects Allāh's commands
Khalīfāh: Caliph
Khuffain: Socks
Kibr: Arrogance
Kuffār: Disbelievers, rejecters
Kufr: Disbelief

L
Lawh-e-Mahfooz: The Sacred Tablet

M
Madhab: School of thought
Makkah: The holiest city of Islam
Masah: Passing wet hands
Masah alal Khuffain: Passing wet hands over leather socks
Masaa'il: Issues/Queries
Masjid: Mosque
Maslak: School of thought
Mā'sūm: Innocent, sinless
Mufassireen: Commentators of the Holy Qur'ān
Muftiyaan e kiraam: People who have studied the course of Iftaa and developed the capacity to deliver legal opinions
Musannifeen: Authors
Mushrikeen: Polytheists, Pagans, idolaters, and disbelievers in the oneness of Allāh
Mustahab: Agreeable, Desirable, Liked
Mutawaatir Ahādīth: Hadīth proven by recurrent testimony

N

Nass Qat'ee: A Piece of text, usually in the Qur'ān, which has a compelling authority, which is undeniable, i.e. denying it will result in Kufr.

Q

Qadhā: Making up for missed prayers
Qisās: Reprisal, Killing as a repayment for murder
Qiyāmah: Day of Judgement
Qur'ān: The final word of God Almighty, compiled in its original form up to this date

R

Radhiallāhū Anhu/ Anha: May Allāh be pleased with him/her
Rahimahullah: May Allāh have mercy upon him
Ramadhān: The ninth month of the Islamic calendar, the month of observing fast
Rasūl: Messenger
Rawaafidh: A sect who claim to love Alī ؓ and that he should have been appointed as a successor to the Prophet ﷺ
Rooh: Soul

S

Sadaqah: Charity, Alms giving
Sahābā: The noble companions of the Holy Prophet ﷺ, who saw him and believed him
Sahīh tradition in text and chain
Salāh Hadīth: Authentic: Prayer
Shari'ah: Islamic code
Shaytān: Devil
Shīā: Deviant sect away from beliefs of mainstream Islam
Shirk: Polytheism, to worship other deity than Allāh

Sihah Sittah: The six authentic books of Hadith. [Bukhārī, Muslim, Abū Dāwūd, Tirmīdhī, Nasai, Ibn Mājah]

Sunnah: Way of the Prophet ﷺ

Sūrah: Chapter of the Qur'ān

T

Tablīgh: Propagation

Tasfīr: Exegesis, most often used to describe the commentary of the Qur'ān

Takabbur: Pride

Taqdeer: Destiny

Taqleed: Following a school of thought, trusting the research of an Imām and his students. There are four schools of thought: Hanafī, Shāfi'ī, Mālikī and Hanbalī.

Taqwā: Piety, constant awareness of Allāh

Tawheed: To confirm the oneness of Allāh

Tawfeeq: To makes easy, give the ability to do something

U

Ulamā: Scholars, Islamic Theologians

Ummah: Nation

Usool: Principles

Ustādh: Teacher

W

Wahm: Delusion/Error

Wudhū: Ablution

Wudhū Khānā: Place of ablution

Z

Zakāh: Charity, 2.5 percent of surplus wealth, which a Muslim should give to the poor once a year

Zimmī: Non-Muslim living under Islamic rule under the protection of Muslims
Zinā: Adultery